OpenStack Administration with Ansible 2

Second Edition

Orchestrate and automate your OpenStack cloud operator tasks with Ansible 2.0

Walter Bentley

BIRMINGHAM - MUMBAI

OpenStack Administration with Ansible 2

Second Edition

Copyright © 2016 Packt Publishing

First published: January 2016

Second edition: December 2016

Production reference: 1221216

Published by Packt Publishing Ltd.
Livery Place
35 Livery Street
Birmingham
B3 2PB, UK.
ISBN 978-1-78712-163-8

www.packtpub.com

Credits

Author
Walter Bentley

Reviewer
Travis Truman

Commissioning Editor
Pratik Shah

Acquisition Editor
Rahul Nair

Content Development Editor
Abhishek Jadhav

Technical Editor
Mohd Riyan Khan

Copy Editor
Dipti Mankame

Project Coordinator
Judie Jose

Proofreader
Safis Editing

Indexer
Francy Puthiry

Graphics
Kirk D'Penha

Production Coordinator
Deepika Naik

About the Author

Walter Bentley is a Rackspace Private Cloud Technical Marketing Engineer and author with a diverse background in production systems administration and solutions architecture. He has more than 15 years of experience in sectors such as online marketing, financial, insurance, aviation, the food industry, education, and now in technology. In the past, he was typically the requestor, consumer, and advisor to companies in the use of technologies such as OpenStack. Today, he's an OpenStack promoter and cloud educator. In his current role, Walter helps customers build, design, and deploy private clouds built on OpenStack. That includes professional services engagements around operating OpenStack clouds and DevOps engagements creating playbooks/roles with Ansible. He presents and speaks regularly at OpenStack Summits, AnsibleFest, and other technology conferences, plus webinars, blog posts and technical reviews. His first book, *OpenStack Administration with Ansible*, was released in 2016.

I would like to thank my wife and best friend Tasha for allowing me to take on this life changing opportunity for the second time around. Without her understanding and support I do not think it could have all happened. She is truly my life's motivation. Also, wish to thank my wonderful daughters, London and Rio, for bringing so much joy to our lives. Thank you to my mother and father for cultivating the technical spirit within me from a very early age (that Commodore 64 was definitely my springboard…LOL).

I would also like to thank my coworker and fellow architect Kevin Jackson for providing me with the courage to take on this project. I also wish to give deep thanks and gratitude to all of my mentors over the years I have had the privilege to work for and with. Those individuals include David Bartlett, Tyrone Paige, Steve Contrabasso, and Mike Childress. Their multitude of great advice has allowed me to be where I am today.

About the Reviewer

Travis Truman has 20+ years of experience in the technology industry. His previous roles include software engineering, software product architecture, SaaS platform architecture, and VP of Engineering in several Philadelphia-area startups. Travis is a regular contributor to open source software and has contributed code to OpenStack, Ansible, GopherCloud, Terraform, Packer, Consul, and many other projects powering modern cloud computing. Travis currently works as a Cloud Architect focused on OpenStack, AWS, and Azure for a Fortune 50 media and technology company based in Philadelphia.

www.PacktPub.com

For support files and downloads related to your book, please visit www.PacktPub.com.

Did you know that Packt offers eBook versions of every book published, with PDF and ePub files available? You can upgrade to the eBook version at www.PacktPub.com and as a print book customer, you are entitled to a discount on the eBook copy. Get in touch with us at service@packtpub.com for more details.

At www.PacktPub.com, you can also read a collection of free technical articles, sign up for a range of free newsletters and receive exclusive discounts and offers on Packt books and eBooks.

https://www.packtpub.com/mapt

Get the most in-demand software skills with Mapt. Mapt gives you full access to all Packt books and video courses, as well as industry-leading tools to help you plan your personal development and advance your career.

Why subscribe?

- Fully searchable across every book published by Packt
- Copy and paste, print, and bookmark content
- On demand and accessible via a web browser

Customer Feedback

Thank you for purchasing this Packt book. We take our commitment to improving our content and products to meet your needs seriously—that's why your feedback is so valuable. Whatever your feelings about your purchase, please consider leaving a review on this book's Amazon page. Not only will this help us, more importantly it will also help others in the community to make an informed decision about the resources that they invest in to learn.

You can also review for us on a regular basis by joining our reviewers' club. **If you're interested in joining, or would like to learn more about the benefits we offer, please contact us**: customerreviews@packtpub.com.

Table of Contents

Preface

As OpenStack has begun to be considered more of a mainstream cloud platform, the challenge of operating it after it is built has become prevalent. While all cloud tasks can be executed via the API or CLI tool on a one-by-one basis, this would not be the best way to handle larger cloud deployments. The need for more of an automated approach to administering OpenStack is now clear. Most organizations are seeking methods to improve business agility and have realized just having a cloud is not enough. Being able to improve application deployments, reduce infrastructure downtime, and eliminate daily manual tasks can only be accomplished through some sort of automation. OpenStack and Ansible will help any organization close that gap. With the many Infrastructure-as-a-Service capabilities OpenStack has to offer coupled with Ansible, an ease of use configuration management tool, assures a more complete cloud implementation.

Whether you are new to OpenStack or a seasoned cloud administrator, this book will aid you in managing your OpenStack cloud once it is all set up. Packed with real-world OpenStack administrative tasks, we will first step through those working examples natively and then transition to walking through instructions on how to automate these tasks using one of the most popular open source automation tools, Ansible.

Ansible has become a market leader in the Open Source orchestration and automation space. With it too being built using Python, similar to OpenStack, it makes for an easy marriage. The ability to leverage existing and/or new OpenStack modules will allow you to quickly move along your playbook creation.

We will start with a brief overview of OpenStack and Ansible, highlighting some best practices. Next, the beginning of each following chapter will allow you to become more familiar with handling Cloud Operator administration tasks such as creating multiple users/tenants, managing containers, customizing your clouds quotas, taking instance snapshots, setting up active-active regions, running cloud health checks, and more. Finally, each chapter will conclude with a step-by-step tutorial on how to automate those tasks with Ansible. As an added bonus, the fully functional Ansible code will be published on GitHub for your reference while reviewing the chapter and/or for later review.

Consider this book to be a 2-for-1 learning experience, a deep OpenStack-based cloud administrative knowledge and familiarity with how Ansible works. As the reader, you will be encouraged to put hands to the keyboard and give the tasks a try.

What this book covers

Chapter 1, *Introduction to OpenStack*, provides the high-level overview of OpenStack and the projects that make up this cloud platform. This introduction will set the level for the reader on the OpenStack components, concepts, and verbiage.

Chapter 2, *Introduction to Ansible*, gives the detailed review of Ansible 2.0, its features, and the best practices to set a solid starting foundation. Also, it will review why leveraging Ansible to automate OpenStack tasks is the easiest option.

Chapter 3, *Creating Multiple Users/Tenants*, guides the reader through the process of creating users and tenants within OpenStack manually and the creation considerations in order to automate such a process using Ansible.

Chapter 4, *Customizing Your Clouds Quotas*, makes you understand what quotas are and how they are used to restrict your cloud resources. It shows the reader how to create quotas manually in OpenStack. After this, it explains how to automate this process with Ansible in order to handle the task for multiple tenants at one time.

Chapter 5, *Snapshot Your Cloud*, teaches how to create snapshots of your cloud instances manually within OpenStack and how to automate this process using Ansible. It explores the power of being able to snapshot all instances within a tenant in one shot.

Chapter 6, *Migrating Instances*, introduces the concept of migrating select instances across compute nodes in the traditional OpenStack method. Then, it demonstrates the required steps to automate this task while grouping instances together and shows the additional options Ansible can offer in handling a task of this matter.

Chapter 7, *Managing Containers on Your Cloud*, takes the reader through a few strategies on how you can automate building and deploying containers running on your OpenStack cloud. There are a few approaches now available, but the key is automating the process so that it is a reuseable function. For each approach, the chapter shows the building blocks of how to accomplish this successfully with OpenStack.

Chapter 8, *Setting up Active-Active Regions*, gives the detailed review of a few use cases of setting up an Active-Active OpenStack cloud regions. With that knowledge, you will then physically learn how to automate this to deploy onto your clouds.

Chapter 9, *Inventory Your Cloud*, explores how the reader can dynamically inventory all the OpenStack cloud user resources with one Ansible playbook. It walks them through the necessary metrics to gather and how that information can be stored for later reference. This is a very powerful tool to have as a cloud administrator/operator.

Chapter 10, *Health Check Your Cloud with Nagios*, demonstrates some useful tips and tricks on how to check the health of your cloud manually and leverage Ansible to set up Nagios and the necessary checks to monitor your cloud. Nagios is one of the leading open source monitoring platforms out there and compliments OpenStack and Ansible very well.

What you need for this book

In order to truly benefit from this book, it is best to have deployed or have access to an OpenStack cloud built using openstack-ansible (OSA) running with the Newton release or better. The OSA deployment method provides an environment that will install both OpenStack and Ansible.

If you plan to deploy any of the other OpenStack distributions, you would still just need to be running the OpenStack Newton release or better. As well as, have Ansible version 2.1 or better installed on the same nodes or on your workstation.

Also, having a good text editor, such as TextWrangler, Notepad++, or Vim, will be very useful if you plan to add to or edit any of the Ansible playbooks/roles found in the GitHub repository.

Who this book is for

If you are an OpenStack-based cloud operator and/or infrastructure administrator with basic OpenStack knowledge already and are interested in automating administrative functions, then this book is exactly what you are looking for. You will take your basic OpenStack knowledge to the next level by learning how to automate simple and advanced OpenStack administration tasks. Having a functioning OpenStack environment is helpful but most certainly not required.

Conventions

In this book, you will find a number of text styles that distinguish between different kinds of information. Here are some examples of these styles and an explanation of their meaning.

Code words in text, database table names, folder names, filenames, file extensions, pathnames, dummy URLs, user input, and Twitter handles are shown as follows: "We can start from the top with the role we created named `create-users-env`."

A block of code is set as follows:

```
- name: User password assignment
  debug: msg="User {{ item.0 }} was added to {{ item.2 }} project, with the
assigned password of {{ item.1 }}"
  with_together:
   - userid
   - passwdss.stdout_lines
   - tenantid
```

When we wish to draw your attention to a particular part of a code block, the relevant lines or items are set in bold:

```
- name: User password assignment
  debug: msg="User {{ item.0 }} was added to {{ item.2 }} project, with the
assigned password of {{ item.1 }}"
  with_together:
   - userid
   - passwdss.stdout_lines
   - tenantid
```

Any command-line input or output is written as follows:

```
$ source openrc
$ openstack user create --password-prompt <username>
```

New terms and **important words** are shown in bold. Words that you see on the screen, for example, in menus or dialog boxes, appear in the text like this: "View them via the **Horizon** dashboard under the **Images** tab."

Warnings or important notes appear in a box like this.

Tips and tricks appear like this.

Reader feedback

Feedback from our readers is always welcome. Let us know what you think about this book-what you liked or disliked. Reader feedback is important for us as it helps us develop titles that you will really get the most out of.

To send us general feedback, simply e-mail `feedback@packtpub.com`, and mention the book's title in the subject of your message.

If there is a topic that you have expertise in and you are interested in either writing or contributing to a book, see our author guide at `www.packtpub.com/authors`.

Customer support

Now that you are the proud owner of a Packt book, we have a number of things to help you to get the most from your purchase.

Downloading the example code

You can download the example code files from your account at `http://www.packtpub.com` for all the Packt Publishing books you have purchased. If you purchased this book elsewhere, you can visit `http://www.packtpub.com/support` and register to have the files e-mailed directly to you.

The complete set of code can also be downloaded from the following GitHub repository: `https://github.com/PacktPublishing/OpenStack-Administration-with-Ansible-2`.

The same code files are available at the author's repository, `https://github.com/os-admin-with-ansible/os-admin-with-ansible-v2`.

Errata

Although we have taken every care to ensure the accuracy of our content, mistakes do happen. If you find a mistake in one of our books-maybe a mistake in the text or the code-we would be grateful if you could report this to us. By doing so, you can save other readers from frustration and help us improve subsequent versions of this book. If you find any errata, please report them by visiting `http://www.packtpub.com/submit-errata`, selecting your book, clicking on the **Errata Submission Form** link, and entering the details of your errata. Once your errata are verified, your submission will be accepted and the errata will be uploaded to our website or added to any list of existing errata under the **Errata** section of that title.

To view the previously submitted errata, go to `https://www.packtpub.com/books/conten t/support`and enter the name of the book in the search field. The required information will appear under the **Errata** section.

Piracy

Piracy of copyrighted material on the Internet is an ongoing problem across all media. At Packt, we take the protection of our copyright and licenses very seriously. If you come across any illegal copies of our works in any form on the Internet, please provide us with the location address or website name immediately so that we can pursue a remedy.

Please contact us at `copyright@packtpub.com` with a link to the suspected pirated material.

We appreciate your help in protecting our authors and our ability to bring you valuable content.

Questions

If you have a problem with any aspect of this book, you can contact us at `questions@packtpub.com`, and we will do our best to address the problem.

1

Introduction to OpenStack

This chapter will serve as a high-level overview of OpenStack and the projects that make up this cloud platform. Laying a clear foundation about OpenStack is very important in order to describe the OpenStack components, concepts, and verbiage. Once the overview is covered, we will transition into discussing the core features and benefits of OpenStack. Finally, the chapter will finish up with two working examples of how you can consume the OpenStack services via the **application program interface** (**API**) and **command-line interface** (**CLI**).

- An overview of OpenStack
- Reviewing the OpenStack services
- OpenStack supporting components
- Features and benefits
- Working examples: listing the services

An overview of OpenStack

In the simplest definition possible, OpenStack can be described as an open source cloud operating platform that can be used to control large pools of compute, storage, and networking resources throughout a data center, all managed through a single interface controlled by either an API, CLI, and/or web **graphical user interface** (**GUI**) dashboard. The power that OpenStack offers administrators is the ability to control all of those resources, while still empowering the cloud consumers to provision those very same resources through other self-service models. OpenStack was built in a modular fashion; the platform is made up of numerous components. Some of those components are considered core services and are required in order to have a function cloud, whereas the other services are optional and only required unless they fit into your personal use case.

The OpenStack Foundation

Back in early 2010, Rackspace was just a technology hosting that focused on providing service and support through an offering named **Fanatical Support**. The company decided to create an open source cloud platform.

The OpenStack Foundation is made up of voluntary members governed by appointed board of directors and project-based tech committees. Collaboration occurs around a six-month, time-based major code release cycle. The release names are run in the alphabetical order and reference the region encompassing the location where the OpenStack design summit will be held. Each release incorporates something called **OpenStack Design Summit**, which is meant to build collaboration among OpenStack operators/consumers, allowing project developers to have live working sessions and also agree on release items.

As an OpenStack Foundation member, you can take an active role in helping develop any of the OpenStack projects. There is no other cloud platform that allows for such participation.

To learn more about the OpenStack Foundation, you can go to the website, `www.openstack.org`.

Reviewing the OpenStack services

Getting to the meat and potatoes of what makes up OpenStack as a project would be to review the services that make up this cloud ecosystem. One thing to keep in mind in reference to the OpenStack services is each service will have an official name and a code name associated with it. The use of the code names has become very popular among the community and most documentation will refer to the services in that manner. Becoming familiar with the code names is important and will ease the adoption process.

The other thing to keep in mind is each service is developed as an API driven REST web service. All actions are executed via that API, enabling for ultimate consumption flexibility. Even when using the CLI or web-based GUI, behind the scenes API calls are being executed and interpreted.

As of the Newton release, the OpenStack project consists of six of what are called **Core Services** and thirteen **Optional Services**. The services will be reviewed in order of release to show an overall services timeline. That timeline will show the natural progression of the OpenStack project overall, also showing how it is now surely Enterprise ready.

A great recent addition provided to the OpenStack community is the creation of **Project Navigator**. The **Project Navigator** is intended to be a living guide to the consumers of the OpenStack projects, aimed to share each of the services community adoption, maturity, and age. Personally, this resource has been found to be very useful and informative. The navigator can be found here on the OpenStack Foundation website, `www.openstack.org/software/project-navigator`.

OpenStack Compute (code-name Nova)

Integrated in release: Austin

Core Service

This was one of the first and is still the most important service part of the OpenStack platform. Nova is the component that provides the bridge to the underlying hypervisor used to manage the computing resources.

> One common misunderstanding is that Nova is a hypervisor in itself, which is simply not true. Nova is a hypervisor manager of sorts, and it is capable of supporting many different types of hypervisors.

Nova would be responsible for scheduling instance creation, sizing options for the instance, managing the instance location, and as mentioned before, keeping track of the hypervisors available to the cloud environment. It also handles the functionality of segregating your cloud into isolation groups named **cells**, **regions**, and **availability zones**.

OpenStack Object Storage (code-name Swift)

Integrated in release: Austin

Core Service

This service was also one of the first services part of the OpenStack platform. Swift is the component that provides **Object Storage as a Service** to your OpenStack cloud, capable of storing petabytes of data, in turn, adding highly available, distributed, and eventually consistent object/blob store. Object storage is intended to be cheap, cost-effective storage solution for static data, such as images, backups, archives, and static content. The objects can then be streamed over standard web protocols (HTTP/S) to or from the object server to the end user initiating the web request. The other key feature to Swift is all data is automatically made highly available as it is replicated across the cluster. The storage cluster is meant to scale horizontally just by simply adding new servers.

OpenStack Image Service (code-name Glance)

Integrated in release: Bextar

Core Service

This service was introduced during the second OpenStack release, and it is responsible for managing/registering/maintaining server images for your OpenStack cloud. It includes the capability to upload or export OpenStack compatible images and store instance snapshots as use as a template/backup for later use. Glance can store those images on a variety of locations, such as locally and/or on distributed storage, for example, object storage. Most Linux kernel distributions already have OpenStack compatible images available for download. You can also create your own server images from existing servers. There exists support for multiple image formats including Raw, VHD, qcow2, VMDK, OVF, and VDI.

OpenStack Identity (code-name Keystone)

Integrated in release: Essex

Core Service

This service was introduced during the fifth OpenStack release. Keystone is the authentication and authorization component built into your OpenStack cloud. Its key role is to handle creation, registry, and management of users, tenants, and all the other OpenStack services. Keystone would be the first component to be installed when standing up an OpenStack cloud. It has the capability to connect to external directory services such as LDAP. Another key feature of Keystone is that it is built based on **role-based access controls** (**RBAC**). Allowing cloud operators to provide distinct role-based access to individual service features to the cloud consumers.

OpenStack Dashboard (code-name Horizon)

Integrated in release: Essex

This service is the second service to be introduced in the fifth OpenStack release. Horizon provides cloud operators and consumers with a web-based GUI to control their compute, storage, and network resources. The OpenStack dashboard runs on top of **Apache** and the **Django** REST framework. Making it very easy to integrate into and extend to meet your personal use case. On the backend, Horizon also uses the native OpenStack APIs. The basis behind Horizon was to be able to provide cloud operators with a quick overall view of the state of their cloud, and cloud consumers a self-service provisioning portal to the clouds resources designated to them.

> Keep in mind that Horizon can handle approximately 70% of the overall available OpenStack functionality. To leverage 100% of the OpenStack functionality, you would need to use the API's directly and/or use CLI for each service.

OpenStack Networking (code-name Neutron)

Integrated in release: Folsom

Core Service

This service is probably the second most powerful component within your OpenStack cloud next to Nova.

> *OpenStack Networking is intended to provide a pluggable, scalable and API-driven system for managing networks and IP addresses.*

This quote was taken directly from the OpenStack Networking documentation as it best reflects exactly the purpose behind Neutron. Neutron is responsible for creating your virtual networks with your OpenStack cloud. This would entail creation of virtual networks, routers, subnets, firewalls, load balancers, and similar network functions. Neutron was developed with an extension framework, which allows for integration from additional network components (physical network device control) and models (flat, Layer 2, and/or Layer 3 networks). Various vendor-specific plugins and adapters have been created to work inline with Neutron. This service adds to the self-service aspect of OpenStack, removing the network aspect from being a roadblock to consuming your cloud.

With Neutron being one of the most advanced and powerful components within OpenStack, a whole book was dedicated to it.

OpenStack Block Storage (code-name Cinder)

Integrated in release: Folsom

Core Service

Cinder is the component that provides **Block Storage as a Service** to your OpenStack cloud by leveraging local disks or attached storage devices. This translates into persistent block-level storage volumes available to your instances. Cinder is responsible for managing and maintaining the block volumes created, attaching/detaching those volumes, and also backup creation of that volume. One of the highly notable features of Cinder is its ability to connect to multiple types of backend-shared storage platforms at the same time. This capabilities spectrum also spans all the way down to being able to leverage simple Linux server storage as well. As an added bonus, **quality of service** (**QoS**) roles can be applied to the different types of backends. Extending the ability to use the block storage devices to meet various application requirements.

OpenStack Orchestration (code-name Heat)

Integrated in release: Havana

This was one of the two services to be introduced in the eighth OpenStack release. Heat provides the orchestration capability over your OpenStack cloud resources. It is described as a mainline project part of the OpenStack orchestration program. This infers that additional automation functionality is in the pipeline for OpenStack.

The built-in orchestration engine is used to automate provisioning of applications and its components, known as a stack. A stack might include instances, networks, subnets, routers, ports, router interfaces, security groups, security group rules, Auto Scaling rules, and so on. Heat utilizes templates to define a stack and is written in a standard markup format, YAML. You will hear of those templates referred to as **HOT** (**Heat Orchestration Template**) templates.

OpenStack Telemetry (code-name Ceilometer)

Integrated in release: Havana

This is the second of the two services introduced in the eighth OpenStack release. Ceilometer collects the cloud usage and performance statistics together into one centralized data store. This capability becomes a key component to a cloud operator as it gives clear metrics into the overall cloud, which can be used to make scaling decisions.

> You have the option of choosing the data store backend to Ceilometer. Such options include MongoDB, MySQL, PostgreSQL, HBase, and DB2.

OpenStack Database (code-name Trove)

Integrated in release: Icehouse

Trove is the component that provides **Database as a Service** to your OpenStack cloud. This capability includes providing scalable and reliable relational and nonrelational database engines. The goal behind this service was to remove the burden of needing to understand database installation and administration. With Trove, cloud consumers can provision database instances just by leveraging the services API. Trove supports multiple singe-tenant databases within a Nova instance.

> The data store types currently supported are MySQL, MongoDB, Cassandra, Redis, and CouchDB.

OpenStack Data Processing (code-name Sahara)

Integrated in release: Juno

Sahara is the component that provides **Data Processing as a Service** to your OpenStack cloud. This capability includes the ability to provision an application cluster tuned to handle large amounts of analytical data. The data store options available are **Hadoop** and/or **Spark**. This service will also aid the cloud consumer in being able to abstract the complication of installing and maintaining this type of cluster.

OpenStack Bare Metal Provisioning (code-name Ironic)

Integrated in release: Kilo

This service has been one of the most anxiously awaited components part of the OpenStack project. Ironic provides the capability to provision physical Bare Metal servers from within your OpenStack cloud. It is commonly known as a Bare Metal hypervisor API and leverages a set of plugins to enable interaction with the Bare Metal servers. It is the newest service to be introduced to the OpenStack family and is still under development.

Other optional services

There are a few additional services still in the early phases of maturity that are listed later. The scope and depth of some of them are still being determined, so it felt best not to possibly misrepresent them here in writing. The bigger takeaway here is the depth of added capability these new services will add to your OpenStack cloud when they are ready.

Code-name	Service
Zaqar	Messaging service
Manila	Share filesystems
Designate	DNS service
Barbican	Key management
Magnum	Containers
Murano	Application catalog
Congress	Governance

OpenStack supporting components

Very similar to any traditional application, there are dependent core components that are pivotal to its functionality and not necessarily the application itself. In the case of the base OpenStack architecture, there are two core components that would be considered the core or backbone of the cloud. OpenStack functionality requires access to an SQL-based backend database service and an **AMQP** (Advanced Message Queuing Protocol) software platform. Just like with any other technology, OpenStack too has base supported reference architectures out there for us to follow. From a database perspective, the common choice will be MySQL and the default AMQP package is **RabbitMQ**. These two dependencies must be installed, configured, and functional before you can start an OpenStack deployment.

There are additional optional software packages that can also be used to provide further stability as part of your cloud design. Information about this management software and further OpenStack architecture details can be found at the following link http://docs.open stack.org/arch-design/generalpurpose-architecture.html.

Features and benefits

The power of OpenStack has been tested true by numerous enterprise-grade organizations, thus gaining the focus of many leading IT companies. As this adoption increases, we will surely see an increase in consumption and additional improved features/functionality. For now, let's review some of OpenStack's features and benefits.

Fully distributed architecture

Every service within the OpenStack platform can be grouped together and/or separated to meet your personal use case. Also as mentioned earlier, only the Core services (Keystone, Nova, and Glance) are required to have a functioning cloud. All other components can be optional. This level of flexibility is something every administrator seeks for an **Infrastructure as a Service (IaaS)** platform.

Using commodity hardware

OpenStack was uniquely designed to accommodate almost any type of hardware. The underlying OS is the only dependency to OpenStack. As long as OpenStack supports the underlying OS and that OS is supported on the particular hardware, you are all set to go! There is no requirement to purchase OEM hardware or even hardware with specific specs. This gives yet another level of deployment flexibility to administrators. A good example of this can be giving your old hardware sitting around in your data center new life within an OpenStack cloud.

Scaling horizontally or vertically

The ability to easily scale your cloud was another key feature to OpenStack. Adding additional compute nodes is as simple as installing the necessary OpenStack services on the new server. The same process is used to expand the OpenStack services control plane as well. Just as with other platforms, you also can add more computing resources to any node as another approach to scaling up.

Meeting high availability requirements

OpenStack is able to certify meeting high availability (99.9%) requirements for its own infrastructure services if implemented via the documented best practices.

Compute isolation and multi-dc Support

Another key feature of OpenStack is the support to handle compute hypervisor isolation and the ability to support multiple OpenStack regions across data centers. Compute isolation includes the ability to separate multiple pools of hypervisors distinguished by hypervisor type, hardware similarity, and/or vCPU ratio.

The ability to support multiple OpenStack regions, which is a complete installation of functioning OpenStack clouds with shared services such as Keystone and Horizon, across data centers is a key function to maintaining highly available infrastructure. This model eases overall cloud administration, allowing a single pane of glass to manage multiple clouds.

Robust role-based access control

All the OpenStack services allow RBAC when assigning authorization to cloud consumers. This gives cloud operators the ability to decide the specific functions allowed by the cloud consumers. Such an example would be to grant a cloud user the ability to create instances, but deny the ability to upload new server images or adjust instance-sizing options.

Working examples – listing the services

So we have covered what OpenStack is, the services that make up OpenStack, and some of the key features of OpenStack. It is only appropriate to show a working example of the OpenStack functionality and the methods available to manage/administer your OpenStack cloud.

To re-emphasize, OpenStack management, administration, and consumption of services can be accomplished via either an API, CLI, and/or web dashboard. When considering some level of automation, the last option of the web dashboard is normally not involved. So for the remainder of this book, we will solely focus on using the OpenStack APIs and CLIs.

Listing the OpenStack services

Now, let's take a look at how you can use either the OpenStack API or CLI to check for the available services active within your cloud.

Via API

The first step in using the OpenStack services is authentication against Keystone. You must always first authenticate (tell the API who you are) and then receive authorization (API ingests your username and determines what predefined task(s) you can execute) based on what your user is allowed to do. That complete process ends in providing you with an authentication token.

Keystone can provide four different types of token formats: UUID, fernet, PKI, and PKIZ. A typical UUID token looks like this `53f7f6ef0cc344b5be706bcc8b1479e1`. Most do not use the PKI token as it is a much longer string and harder to work with. There are great performance benefits from using fernet tokens instead of UUID due to not requiring persistence. It is suggested to set Keystone to provide fernet tokens within your cloud.

Here is an example of making an authentication request for a secure token. Making API requests using cURL, a useful tool for interacting with RESTful APIs, is the easiest approach. Using cURL with various options, you are able to simulate actions similar to using the OpenStack CLI or the Horizon dashboard:

```
$ curl -d @credentials.json -X POST -H "Content-Type: application/json"
  http://127.0.0.1:5000/v3/auth/tokens | python -mjson.tool
```

Because the credential string is fairly long and easy to incorrectly manipulate, it is suggested to use the -d @<filename> functionality part of cURL. This allows you to insert the credential string into a file and then be able to pass it into your API request by just referencing the file. This exercise is very similar to creating a client environment script (also known as OpenRC files).

Adding | python -mjson.tool to the end of your API request makes the JSON output easier to read.

An example of the credential string would look like this:

```
{
    "auth": {
        "identity": {
            "methods": [
                "password"
            ],
            "password": {
                "user": {
                    "name": "admin",
                    "domain": {
                        "id": "default"
                    },
                    "password": "passwd"
                }
            }
        }
    }
}
```

Downloading the example code

Detailed steps to download the code bundle are mentioned in the Preface of this book.

The code bundle for the book is also hosted on GitHub at: `https://github.com/PacktPublishing/OpenStack-Administration-with-Ansible-2`. We also have other code bundles from our rich catalog of books and videos available at: `https://github.com/PacktPublishing/`. Check them out!

When the example is executed against the Keystone API, it will respond with an authentication token. The token is actually returned within the HTTP header of the response. That token should be used for all subsequent API requests. Keep in mind that the token does expire, but traditionally, a token is configured to the last 24 hours from the creation timestamp.

As mentioned earlier, the token can be found in the HTTP header of the API response message. The HTTP header property name is `X-Subject-Token`:

```
HTTP/1.1 201 Created
Date: Tue, 20 Sep 2016 21:20:02 GMT
Server: Apache
X-Subject-Token:
gAAAAABX4agC32nymQSbku39x1QPooKDpU2T9oPYapF6ZeY4QSA9EOqQZ8PcKqMT2j5m9uvOtC9
c8d9szObciFr06stGo19tNueHDfvHbgRLFmjTg2k8Scu1Q4esvjbwth8aQ-
qMSe4NRTWmD642i6pDfk_AIIQCNA
Vary: X-Auth-Token
x-openstack-request-id: req-8de6fa59-8256-4a07-b040-c21c4aee6064
Content-Length: 283
Content-Type: application/json
```

Once you have the authentication token, you can begin crafting subsequent API requests to request information about your cloud and/or execute tasks. Now we will request the list of services available to your cloud:

```
$ curl -X GET http://127.0.0.1:35357/v3/services -H
  "Accept: application/json" -H "X-Auth-
  Token: 907ca229af164a09918a661ffa224747" | python -mjson.tool
```

The output from this API request will be the complete list of services registered within your cloud by `name`, `description`, `type`, `id`, and whether it is active. An abstract of the output would look similar to the following code:

```
{
  "links": {
    "next": null,
```

```
    "previous": null,
    "self": "http://example.com/identity/v3/services"
  },
  "services": [
    {
      "description": "Nova Compute Service",
      "enabled": true,
      "id": "1999c3a858c7408fb586817620695098",
      "links": {
        "...
      },
      "name": "nova",
      "type": "compute"
    },
    {
      "description": "Cinder Volume Service V2",
      "enabled": true,
      "id": "39216610e75547f1883037e11976fc0f",
      "links": {
        "...
      },
      "name": "cinderv2",
      "type": "volumev2"
    },
  ...
```

Via CLI

All the base principles applied to using the API earlier also applies to using the CLI. The major difference is with the CLI all you need to do is create an OpenRC file with your credentials and execute defined commands. The CLI handles formatting the API calls behind the scenes, grabbing the token for subsequent requests, and formatting the output also.

Same as earlier, first you need to authenticate against Keystone to be granted a secure token. This action is accomplished by first sourcing your OpenRC file and then by executing the `service-list` command. The next example will demonstrate it in more detail. Now that there are two active versions of the Keystone service, version 2.0 and 3.0, you have the choice of which version you wish to have active to handle authentication/authorization.

Here is an example of an OpenRC file v2.0 named `openrc`:

```
# To use an OpenStack cloud you need to authenticate against keystone.
export OS_ENDPOINT_TYPE=internalURL
export OS_USERNAME=admin
```

```
export OS_TENANT_NAME=admin
export OS_AUTH_URL=http://127.0.0.1:5000/v2.0

# With Keystone you pass the keystone password.
echo "Please enter your OpenStack Password: "
read -sr OS_PASSWORD_INPUT
export OS_PASSWORD=$OS_PASSWORD_INPUT
```

The OpenRC file v3.0 would look similar to this:

```
# *NOTE*: Using the 3 *Identity API* does not necessarily mean any other
# OpenStack API is version 3. For example, your cloud provider may
implement
# Image API v1.1, Block Storage API v2, and Compute API v2.0. OS_AUTH_URL
is
# only for the Identity API served through keystone.
export OS_AUTH_URL=http://172.29.238.2:5000/v3

# With the addition of Keystone we have standardized on the term
**project**
# as the entity that owns the resources.
export OS_PROJECT_ID=5408dd3366e943b694cae90a04d71c88
export OS_PROJECT_NAME="admin"
export OS_USER_DOMAIN_NAME="Default"
if [ -z "$OS_USER_DOMAIN_NAME" ]; then unset OS_USER_DOMAIN_NAME; fi

# unset v2.0 items in case set
unset OS_TENANT_ID
unset OS_TENANT_NAME

# In addition to the owning entity (tenant), OpenStack stores the entity
# performing the action as the **user**.
export OS_USERNAME="admin"

# With Keystone you pass the keystone password.
echo "Please enter your OpenStack Password: "
read -sr OS_PASSWORD_INPUT
export OS_PASSWORD=$OS_PASSWORD_INPUT

# If your configuration has multiple regions, we set that information here.
# OS_REGION_NAME is optional and only valid in certain environments.
export OS_REGION_NAME="RegionOne"
# Don't leave a blank variable, unset it if it was empty
if [ -z "$OS_REGION_NAME" ]; then unset OS_REGION_NAME; fi
```

Once you create and source the OpenRC file, you can begin using the CLI to execute commands such as requesting the list of services. Take a look at the following working example:

```
$ source openrc
$ openstack service list
```

The output will look similar to this:

Summary

The adoption of OpenStack among the enterprises has taken off since the first revision of this book. Many large companies such as Walmart, BMW, Volkswagon, AT&T and Comcast have come forward sharing their success stories and continued support for OpenStack. I hope this chapter may have cleared up any questions you had about OpenStack and maybe even dispelled any myths you may have heard.

We will now transition to learning about Ansible and why using it in conjunction with OpenStack is a great combination.

2

Introduction to Ansible

This chapter will serve as a high-level overview of Ansible 2.0 and components that make up this open source configuration management tool. We will cover the definition of the Ansible components and their typical use. Also, we will discuss how to define variables for the roles and defining/setting facts about the hosts for the playbooks. Next, we will transition into how to set up your Ansible environment and the ways you can define the host inventory used to run your playbooks against. We will then cover some of the new components introduced in Ansible 2.0 named **Blocks** and **Strategies**. We will also discuss the cloud modules natively part of the Ansible framework. Finally, the chapter will finish up with a working example of a playbook that will confirm the required host connectivity needed to use Ansible. The following topics will be covered:

- Ansible 2.0 overview.
- What are playbooks, roles, and modules?
- Setting up the environment.
- Variables and facts.
- Defining the inventory.
- Blocks and Strategies.
- Cloud integrations.

Ansible 2.0 overview

Ansible in its simplest form has been described as a Python-based open source IT automation tool that can be used to configure\manage systems, deploy software (or almost anything), and provide orchestration to a process. These are just a few of the many possible use cases for Ansible. In my previous life as a production support infrastructure engineer, I wish such a tool would have existed. I would have surely had much more sleep and a lot less gray hairs.

One thing that always stood out to me in regard to Ansible is that the developer's first and foremost goal was to create a tool that offers simplicity and maximum ease of use. In a world filled with complicated and intricate software, keeping it simple goes a long way for most IT professionals.

Staying with the goal of keeping things simple, Ansible handles configuration/management of hosts solely through **Secure Shell** (**SSH**). Absolutely no daemon or agent is required. The server or workstation where you run the playbooks from only needs Python and a few other packages, most likely already present, installed. Honestly, it does not get simpler than that.

The automation code used with Ansible is organized into something named playbooks and roles, of which is written in YAML markup format. Ansible follows the YAML formatting and structure within the playbooks/roles. Being familiar with YAML formatting helps in creating your playbooks/roles. If you are not familiar do not worry, as it is very easy to pick up (it is all about the spaces and dashes).

The playbooks and roles are in a noncomplied format, making the code very simple to read if familiar with standard Unix\Linux commands. There is also a suggested directory structure in order to create playbooks. This also is one of my favorite features of Ansible. Enabling the ability to review and/or use playbooks written by anyone else with little to no direction needed.

 It is strongly suggested that you review the Ansible playbook best practices before getting started: `http://docs.ansible.com/playbooks_b est_practices.html`. I also find the overall Ansible website very intuitive and filled with great examples at `http://docs.ansible.com`.

My favorite excerpt from the Ansible playbook best practices is under the *Content Organization* section. Having a clear understanding of how to organize your automation code proved very helpful to me. The suggested directory layout for playbooks is as follows:

```
group_vars/
   group1              # here we assign variables to particular groups
   group2              # ""
host_vars/
   hostname1           # if systems need specific variables, put them here
   hostname2           # ""
library/               # if any custom modules, put them here (optional)
filter_plugins/        # if any custom filter plugins, put them here
                          (optional)
site.yml               # master playbook
webservers.yml            # playbook for webserver tier
dbservers.yml          # playbook for dbserver tier
roles/
```

```
common/               # this hierarchy represents a "role"
  tasks/              #
    main.yml          # <-- tasks file can include smaller files if
                            warranted
  handlers/           #
    main.yml          # <-- handlers file
  templates/          # <-- files for use with the template resource
    ntp.conf.j2       # <------- templates end in .j2
  files/              #
    bar.txt           # <-- files for use with the copy resource
    foo.sh            # <-- script files for use with the script resource
  vars/               #
    main.yml          # <-- variables associated with this role
  defaults/           #
    main.yml          # <-- default lower priority variables for this role
  meta/               #
    main.yml          # <-- role dependencies
```

It is now time to dig deeper into reviewing what playbooks, roles, and modules consist of. This is where we will break down each of these component's distinct purposes.

What are playbooks, roles, and modules?

The automation code you will create to be run by Ansible is broken down in hierarchical layers. Envision a pyramid with its multiple levels of elevation. We will start at the top and discuss playbooks first.

Playbooks

Imagine that a playbook is the very topmost triangle of the pyramid. A playbook takes on the role of executing all of the lower level code contained in a role. It can also be seen as a wrapper to the roles created. We will cover the roles in the next section.

Playbooks also contain other high-level runtime parameters, such as the host(s) to run the playbook against, the root user to use, and/or if the playbook needs to be run as a sudo user. These are just a few of the many playbook parameters you can add. Following is an example of what the syntax of a playbook looks like:

```
---
# Sample playbooks structure/syntax.

- hosts: dbservers
  remote_user: root
```

```
become: true
roles:
 - mysql-install
```

 In the preceding example, you will note that the playbook begins with ---
. This is required as the heading (line 1) for each playbook and role.
Also, please note the spacing structure at the beginning of each line. The
easiest way to remember it is each main command starts with a dash (–).
Then, every subcommand starts with two spaces and repeats the lower in
the code hierarchy you go. As we walk through more examples, it will
start to make more sense.

Let's step through the preceding example and break down the sections. The first step in the
playbook was to define what hosts to run the playbook against; in this case, it was
dbservers (which can be a single host or list of hosts). The next area sets the user to run
the playbook as locally, remotely, and it enables executing the playbook as sudo. The last
section of the syntax lists the roles to be executed.

The earlier example is similar to the formatting of the other playbooks you will see in the
next chapters. This format incorporates defining roles, which allows for scaling out
playbooks and reusability (you will find the most advanced playbooks structured this way).
With Ansible's high level of flexibility, you can also create playbooks in a simpler
consolidated format. An example of such kind is as follows:

```
---
# Sample simple playbooks structure/syntax

- name: Install MySQL Playbook
  hosts: dbservers
  remote_user: root
  become: true
  tasks:
   - name: Install MySQL
     apt: name={{item}} state=present
     with_items:
      - libselinux-python
      - mysql
      - mysql-server
      - MySQL-python

   - name: Copying my.cnf configuration file
     template: src=cust_my.cnf dest=/etc/my.cnf mode=0755

   - name: Prep MySQL db
     command: chdir=/usr/bin mysql_install_db
```

```
- name: Enable MySQL to be started at boot
  service: name=mysqld enabled=yes state=restarted

- name: Prep MySQL db
  command: chdir=/usr/bin mysqladmin -u root password 'passwd'
```

Now that we have reviewed what playbooks are, we will move on to reviewing roles and their benefits.

Roles

Moving down to the next level of the Ansible pyramid, we will discuss roles. The most effective way to describe roles is the breaking up a playbook into multiple smaller files. So, instead of having one long playbook with multiple tasks defined, all handling separately related steps, you can break the playbook into individual specific roles. This format keeps your playbooks simple and leads to the ability to reuse roles between playbooks.

 The best advice I personally received concerning creating roles is to keep them simple. Try to create a role to do a specific function, such as just installing a software package. You can then create a second role to just do configurations. In this format, you can reuse the initial installation role over and over without needing to make code changes for the next project.

The typical syntax of a role can be found here and would be placed into a file named `main.yml` within the `roles/<name of role>/tasks` directory:

```
---
- name: Install MySQL
  apt: name="{{ item }}" state=present
  with_items:
    - libselinux-python
    - mysql
    - mysql-server
    - MySQL-python

- name: Copying my.cnf configuration file
  template: src=cust_my.cnf dest=/etc/my.cnf mode=0755

- name: Prep MySQL db
  command: chdir=/usr/bin mysql_install_db

- name: Enable MySQL to be started at boot
  service: name=mysqld enabled=yes state=restarted

- name: Prep MySQL db
```

```
command: chdir=/usr/bin mysqladmin -u root password 'passwd'
```

The complete structure of a role is identified in the directory layout found in the Ansible overview section of this chapter. In the next chapters, we will review additional functions of roles as we step through the working examples. With having covered playbooks and roles, we are prepared to cover the last topic in this session, which are modules.

Modules

Another key feature of Ansible is that it comes with predefined code that can control system functions, named modules. The modules are executed directly against the remote host(s) or via playbooks. The execution of a module generally requires you to pass a set number of arguments. The Ansible website (`http://docs.ansible.com/modules_by_category.html`) does a great job of documenting every available module and the possible arguments to pass to that module.

> The documentation for each module can also be accessed via the command line by executing the `ansible-doc <module name>` command.

The use of modules will always be the recommended approach within Ansible as they are written to avoid making the requested change to the host unless the change needs to be made. This is very useful when re-executing a playbook against a host more than once. The modules are smart enough to know not to re-execute any steps that have already completed successfully, unless some argument or command is changed.

Another thing worth noting is with every new release of Ansible additional modules are introduced. Personally, there was an exciting addition to Ansible 2.0, and these are the updated and extended set of modules set to ease the management of your OpenStack cloud.

Referring back to the previous role example shared earlier, you will note the use of various modules. The modules used are highlighted here again to provide further clarity:

```
---
- name: Install MySQL
  apt: name="{{ item }}" state=present
  with_items:
   - libselinux-python
   - mysql
   - mysql-server
   - MySQL-python
- name: Copying my.cnf configuration file
```

```
    template: src=cust_my.cnf dest=/etc/my.cnf mode=0755
  - name: Prep MySQL db
    command: chdir=/usr/bin mysql_install_db
  - name: Enable MySQL to be started at boot
    service: name=mysqld enabled=yes state=restarted
  ...
```

Another feature worth mentioning is that you are able to not only use the current modules, but you can also write your very own modules. Although the core of Ansible is written in Python, your modules can be written in almost any language. Underneath it, all the modules technically return JSON format data, thus allowing for the language flexibility.

In this section, we were able to cover the top two sections of our Ansible pyramid, playbooks and roles. We also reviewed the use of modules, that is, the built-in power behind Ansible. Next, we transition into another key features of Ansible-variable substitution and gathering host facts.

Setting up the environment

Before you can start experimenting with Ansible, you must install it first. There was no need in duplicating all the great documentation to accomplish this already created on `http://docs.ansible.com/` . I would encourage you to go to the following URL and choose an install method of your choice: `http://docs.ansible.com/ansible/intro_inst allation.html`.

> If you are installing Ansible on Mac OS, I found using Homebrew was much simpler and consistent. More details on using Homebrew can be found at `http://brew.sh`.
> The command to install Ansible with Homebrew is `brew install ansible`.

Upgrading to Ansible 2.0

It is very important to note that in order to use the new features part of Ansible version 2.0, you must update the version running on your OSA deployment node. The version currently running on the deployment node is either 1.9.4 or 1.9.5. The method that seemed to work well every time is outlined here. This part is a bit experimental, so please make a note of any warnings or errors incurred.

From the deployment node, execute the following commands:

```
$ pip uninstall -y ansible
$ sed -i 's/^export ANSIBLE_GIT_RELEASE.*/export
  ANSIBLE_GIT_RELEASE=${ANSIBLE_GIT_RELEASE:-"v2.1.1.0-1"}/' /opt/
  openstack-ansible/scripts/bootstrap-ansible.sh
$ cd /opt/openstack-ansible
$ ./scripts/bootstrap-ansible.sh
```

New OpenStack client authentication

Alongside of the introduction of the new **python-openstackclient**, CLI was the unveiling of the os-client-config library. This library offers an additional way to provide/configure authentication credentials for your cloud. The new OpenStack modules part of Ansible 2.0 leverages this new library through a package named shade. Through the use of os-client-config and shade, you can now manage multiple cloud credentials within a single file named clouds.yaml. When deploying OSA, I discovered that shade will search for this file in the $HOME/.config/openstack/ directory wherever the playbook/role and CLI command is executed. A working example of the clouds.yaml file is shown as follows:

```
# Ansible managed:
  /etc/ansible/roles/openstack_openrc/templates/clouds.yaml.j2 modified
    on 2016-06-16 14:00:03 by root on 082108-allinone02
clouds:
 default:
  auth:
   auth_url: http://172.29.238.2:5000/v3
   project_name: admin
   tenant_name: admin
   username: admin
   password: passwd
   user_domain_name: Default
   project_domain_name: Default
  region_name: RegionOne
  interface: internal
  identity_api_version: "3"
```

Using this new authentication method drastically simplifies creating automation code to work on an OpenStack environment. Instead of passing a series of authentication parameters in line with the command, you can just pass a single parameter, `--os-cloud=default`. The Ansible OpenStack modules can also use this new authentication method, and you will note that most examples in the coming chapters will use this option. More details about `os-client-config` can be found at: `http://docs.openstack.org/developer/os-client-config`.

> Installing shade is required to use the Ansible OpenStack modules in version 2.0. Shade will be required to be installed directly on the deployment node and the Utility container (if you decide to use this option). If you encounter problems installing shade, try the `-pip install shade-isolated` command.

Variables and facts

Anyone who has ever attempted to create some sort of automation code, whether via **bash** or **Perl** scripts, knows that being able to define variables is an essential component. Like other programming languages Ansible does contain features such as variable substitution.

Variables

To start, let's first define the meaning of variables and use in the event this is a new concept.

> *Variable (computer science), a symbolic name associated with a value and whose associated value may be changed*

Using variables allows you to set a symbolic placeholder in your automation code that you can substitute values for on each execution. Ansible accommodates defining variables within your playbooks and roles in various ways. When dealing with OpenStack and/or cloud technologies in general, being able to adjust your execution parameters on the fly is critical.

We will step through a few ways of how you can set variable placeholders in your playbooks, how to define variable values, and how you can register the result of a task as a variable.

Setting variable placeholders

In the event you wanted to set a variable placeholder within your playbooks, you would add the following syntax like this:

```
- name: Copying my.cnf configuration file
  template: src=cust_my.cnf dest={{ CONFIG_LOC }} mode=0755
```

In the preceding example, the CONFIG_LOC variable was added in the place of the configuration file location (/etc/my.cnf) designated in the earlier example. When setting the placeholder, the variable name must be encased within {{ }} as shown in the preceding example.

Defining variable values

Now that you have added the variable to your playbook, you must define the variable value. This can be done easily by passing command-line values as follows:

```
$ ansible-playbook base.yml --extra-vars "CONFIG_LOC=/etc/my.cnf"
```

Or you can define the values directly in your playbook, within each role or include them inside of global playbook variable files. Here are the examples of the three options.

Define a variable value directly in your playbook by adding the vars section:

```
---
# Sample simple playbooks structure/syntax

- name: Install MySQL Playbook
  hosts: dbservers
  ...
  vars:
    CONFIG_LOC: /etc/my.cnf
  ...
```

Define a variable value within each role by creating a variable file named main.yml within the vars/ directory of the role with the following contents:

```
---
CONFIG_LOC: /etc/my.cnf
```

To define the variable value inside of the global playbook, you would first create a host-specific variable file within the `group_vars/` directory in the root of the playbook directory with the exact same contents as mentioned earlier. In this case, the variable file must be named to match the host or host group name defined within the `hosts` file.

As in the earlier example, the host group name is `dbservers`; in turn, a file named `dbservers` would be created within the `group_vars/` directory.

Registering variables

The situation at times arises when you want to capture the output of a task. Within the process of capturing the result you are in essence registering a dynamic variable. This type of variable is slightly different from the standard variables we have covered so far.

Here is an example of registering the result of a task to a variable:

```
- name: Check Keystone process
  shell: ps -ef | grep keystone
  register: keystone_check
```

The registered variable value data structure can be stored in a few formats. It will always follow a base JSON format, but the value can be stored under different attributes. Personally, I have found it difficult at times to blindly determine the format. The tip given here will save you hours of troubleshooting.

To review and have the data structure of a registered variable returned when running a playbook, you can use the `debug` module, such as adding this to the previous example: `- debug: var=keystone_check`.

Facts

When Ansible runs a playbook, one of the first things it does on your behalf is gather facts about the host before executing tasks or roles. The information gathered about the host will range from the base information such as operating system and IP addresses to the detailed information such as the hardware type/resources. The details captured are then stored into a variable named facts.

You can find a complete list of available facts on the Ansible website at: `http://docs.ansible.com/playbooks_variables.html#information-discovered-from-systems-facts`.

You have the option to disable the facts gather process by adding the following to your playbook: `gather_facts: false`. Facts about a host are captured by default unless the feature is disabled.

A quick way of viewing all facts associated with a host, you can manually execute the following via a command line:

```
$ ansible dbservers -m setup
```

There is plenty more you can do with facts, and I would encourage you to take some time reviewing them in the Ansible documentation. Next, we will learn more about the base of our pyramid, the host inventory. Without an inventory of hosts to run the playbooks against, you would be creating the automation code for nothing.

So to close out this chapter, we will dig deeper into how Ansible handles host inventory, whether it be in a static and/or dynamic format.

Defining the inventory

The process of defining a collection of hosts to Ansible is named the **inventory**. A host can be defined using its **fully qualified domain name** (**FQDN**), local hostname, and/or its IP address. Since Ansible uses SSH to connect to the hosts, you can provide any alias for the host that the machine where Ansible is installed can understand.

Ansible expects the `inventory` file to be in an INI-like format and named hosts. By default, the `inventory` file is usually located in the `/etc/ansible` directory and will look as follows:

```
athena.example.com

[ocean]
aegaeon.example.com
ceto.example.com

[air]
aeolus.example.com
zeus.example.com
apollo.example.com
```

Personally, I have found the default `inventory` file to be located in different places depending on the operating system Ansible is installed on. With that point, I prefer to use the `-i` command-line option when executing a playbook. This allows me to designate the specific `hosts` file location. A working example would look like this: `ansible-playbook -i hosts base.yml`.

In the preceding example, there is a single host and a group of hosts defined. The hosts are grouped together into a group by defining a group name enclosed in `[ ]` inside the `inventory` file. Two groups are defined in the earlier mentioned example `ocean` and `air`.

In the event where you do not have any hosts within your `inventory` file (such as in the case of running a playbook locally only), you can add the following entry to define localhost like this:

```
[localhost]
localhost ansible_connection=local
```

The option exists to define variable for hosts and a group inside of your `inventory` file. More information on how to do this and additional inventory details can be found on the Ansible website at `http://docs.ansible.com/intro_inventory.html`.

Dynamic inventory

It seemed appropriate since we are automating functions on a cloud platform to review yet another great feature of Ansible, which is the ability to dynamically capture an inventory of hosts/instances. One of the primary principles of cloud is to be able to create instances on demand directly via an API, GUI, CLI, and/or through automation code, like Ansible. That basic principle will make relying on a static `inventory` file pretty much a useless choice. This is why you will need to rely heavily on dynamic inventory.

A dynamic inventory script can be created to pull information from your cloud at runtime and then, in turn, use that information for the playbooks execution. Ansible provides the functionality to detect if an `inventory` file is set as an executable and if so will execute the script to pull current time inventory data.

Since creating an Ansible dynamic inventory script is considered more of an advanced activity, I am going to direct you to the Ansible website, (`http://docs.ansible.com/intro _dynamic_inventory.html`), as they have a few working examples of dynamic inventory scripts there.

Fortunately, in our case, we will be reviewing an OpenStack cloud built using the **openstack-ansible (OSA)** repository. OSA comes with a prebuilt dynamic inventory script that will work for your OpenStack cloud. That script is named `dynamic_inventory.py` and can be found within the `playbooks/inventory` directory located in the `root OSA deployment` folder. In the follwoing chapters, you will see working examples of how to leverage this dynamic `inventory` file. A simple example of how to use the dynamic `inventory` file is given later.

First, execute the dynamic `inventory` script manually to become familiar with the data structure and group names defined (this example assumes that you are in the `root OSA deployment` directory):

```
$ cd playbooks/inventory
$ ./dynamic_inventory.py
```

This will print to the screen an output similar to this:

```
...
},
   "compute_all": {
     "hosts": [
        "compute1_rsyslog_container-19482f86",
        "compute1",
        "compute2_rsyslog_container-dee00ea5",
        "compute2"
     ]
   },
   "utility_container": {
     "hosts": [
        "infra1_utility_container-c5589031"
     ]
   },
   "nova_spice_console": {
     "hosts": [
        "infra1_nova_spice_console_container-dd12200f"
     ],
     "children": []
   },
...
```

Next, with this information, you now know that if you wanted to run a playbook against the utility container, all you would have to do is execute the playbook like this:

```
$ ansible-playbook -i inventory/dynamic_inventory.py playbooks/base.yml -l
  utility_container
```

In this section, we will cover two new features added to version 2.0 of Ansible. Both features add additional functionality to how tasks are grouped or executed within a playbook. So far, they seem to be really nice features when creating more complex automation code. We will now briefly review each of the two new features.

Blocks

The Block feature can simply be explained as a way of logically grouping tasks together with the option of also applying customized error handling. It gives the option to group a set of tasks together, establishing specific conditions and privileges. An example of applying the Block functionality to an earlier example can be found here:

```
---
# Sample simple playbooks structure/syntax

- name: Install MySQL Playbook
  hosts: dbservers
  tasks:
   - block:
     - apt: name={{item}} state=present
       with_items:
         - libselinux-python
         - mysql
         - mysql-server
         - MySQL-python

     - template: src=cust_my.cnf dest=/etc/my.cnf mode=0755

     - command: chdir=/usr/bin mysql_install_db

     - service: name=mysqld enabled=yes state=restarted

     - command: chdir=/usr/bin mysqladmin -u root password 'passwd'
   when: ansible_distribution == 'Ubuntu'
   remote_user: root
   become: true
```

Additional details on how to implement Blocks and any associated error handling can be found at http://docs.ansible.com/ansible/playbooks_blocks.html.

Strategies

The **strategy** feature allows you to add control on how a play is executed by the hosts. Currently, the default behavior is described as being the linear strategy, where all hosts will execute each task before any host moves on to the next task. As of today, the two other strategy types that exist are free and debug. Since Strategies are implemented as a new type of plugin to Ansible, more can be easily added by contributing code. Additional details on Strategies can be found at `http://docs.ansible.com/ansible/playbooks_strategies.html`.

A simple example of implementing a strategy within a playbook is as follows:

```
---
# Sample simple playbooks structure/syntax

- name: Install MySQL Playbook
  hosts: dbservers
  strategy: free
  tasks:
  ...
```

The new debug strategy is extremely helpful when you need to step through your playbook/role to find something like a missing variable, determine what variable value to supply, or figure out why it may be sporadically failing. These are just a few of the possible use cases. Definitely I encourage you to give this feature a try. Here is the URL to more details on the playbook debugger: `http://docs.ansible.com/ansible/playbooks_debugger.html`.

Cloud integrations

Since cloud automation is the main and most important theme of this book, it only makes sense that we highlight the many different cloud integrations Ansible 2.0 offers right out of the box. Again, this was one of the reasons why I immediately fell in love with Ansible. Yes, the other automation tools also have hooks into many of the cloud providers, but I found at times they did not work or were not mature enough to leverage. Ansible has gone above and beyond to not fall into that trap. Not saying Ansible has all the bases covered, it does feel like most are and that is what matters most to me.

If you have not checked out the cloud modules available for Ansible, take a moment now and take a look at `http://docs.ansible.com/ansible/list_of_cloud_modules.html`. From time to time check back, as I am confident that you will be surprised to find more have been added. I am very proud of my Ansible family for keeping on top of these and making it much easier to write automation code against our clouds.

Specific to OpenStack, a bunch of new modules have been added to the Ansible library as of version 2.0. The extensive list can be found at `http://docs.ansible.com/ansible/list_of_cloud_modules.html#openstack`. You will note that the biggest changes, from the first version of this book to this one, will be focused on using as many of the new OpenStack modules when possible.

Summary

Let's pause here on exploring the dynamic `inventory` script capabilities and continue to build upon it as we dissect the working examples in the following chapters.

Personally, I am very excited to move to the next chapter where we will create our very first OpenStack administration playbook together. We will start off with a fairly simple task of creating users and tenants. This will also include reviewing a few automation considerations that you will need to keep in mind when creating automation code for OpenStack. Ready? Ok, let's get started!

3
Creating Multiple Users/Projects

We have finally arrived to the part of the book where we put hands to the keyboard and create our very first OpenStack administration playbook. The task of creating users and projects for your OpenStack cloud is literally one of the first steps in setting up your cloud for user consumption. So, it is good to start here. We will step through how one would manually do this first and then transition into creating a playbook with roles to fully automate it. While creating the playbook/role, I will try to highlight any possible concerns and flexible ways you can accomplish it using Ansible. The following topics will be covered in this chapter:

- Creating users and projects
- Automation considerations
- Coding the playbook and roles
- Playbook and role review

Creating users and projects

Although creating new users and projects seems like a trivial task as a cloud operator/administrator, it does become a burden if asked to create 10, 20, or 50 users and 5, 10, or 20 projects. The process of first creating the user (with a corresponding complex secure password), next creating the project for the user, and finally linking that user to that project while assigning that user with the appropriate role.

Imagine doing that over and over again. Boring! The first thing you learn as an administrator of anything is: figure out what your daily tasks are and then determine how to get them completed as fast/easily as possible. This is exactly what we are going to do here.

Manually creating users and projects

To further demonstrate the steps outlined earlier, we will walk through the commands used to create a user and a project.

> For simplicity purposes, we will demonstrate the manual commands using the OpenStack CLI only.

Creating a user

Creating a user within OpenStack involves sending requests to the Identity service (Keystone). The Keystone request can be executed by either first sourcing the OpenRC file discussed in Chapter 1, *Introduction to OpenStack* or by passing the --os-cloud authentication parameter in line with the command (this is shown in the second example later). Next, you would be responsible for providing the required parameter values such as the user name and password with the command. See the following example:

```
$ source openrc
$ openstack user create --password-prompt <username>
```

Or we can also use this:

```
$ openstack --os-cloud=<cloud name> user create --password-prompt
  <username>
```

The output will look similar to this:

```
root@allinone-utility-container-fdb175b5:~# openstack --os-cloud=default user create --password-prompt test_user
User Password:
Repeat User Password:
+-----------+----------------------------------+
| Field     | Value                            |
+-----------+----------------------------------+
| domain_id | default                          |
| enabled   | True                             |
| id        | c3f7d0fd249b4e16a0d1fe6911659797 |
| name      | test_user                        |
+-----------+----------------------------------+
root@allinone-utility-container-fdb175b5:~#
```

Creating a project

As touched on previously, a project (formerly known as a tenant) is a segregated area of your cloud where you can assign users. That user can be restricted to just that project or allowed access to multiple projects. The process of creating a project is similar to the user creation process mentioned earlier. You can continue to execute CLI commands once you source the OpenRC file or pass an authentication parameter with each command. Imagine that the OpenRC file was already sourced, see the following example:

```
$ openstack --os-cloud=<cloud name> project create
  --description="<project description>" <project name>
```

The output will look similar to this:

Assigning a role and project access to users

Still using the Keystone service, you would assign a specific role (user permissions) to a designated project for the user just created. There are default roles that come with a base OpenStack cloud: `admin` and `_member_`. You can also create custom roles as well. You would need the name of the role and project you wish to assign to the user. If the OpenRC file was still sourced, see the following example. For this command no output is printed to the screen:

```
$ openstack role add --user=<username> --project=<project name> <role name>
```

At this point, you would have created a user and a project and have assigned that user to the project with a role, which is all done manually. Let's move forward into reviewing some of the considerations around the thought of automating all the steps mentioned earlier.

Automation considerations

The idea of taking a manual task and creating an automation script, no matter the automation tool, requires some base framework decisions to be made. This is to keep consistency within your code and allow the easy adoption of your code by someone else. Have you ever tried using scripts created by someone else and they had no code standards? It is confusing, and you waste time attempting to understand their approach.

In our case, we are going to make some framework decisions ahead of time and keep that consistency. My biggest disclaimer before we get started reviewing the considerations in order to set our framework decisions is:

> There are many ways to approach automating tasks for OpenStack with Ansible; the one shown in this book is just one way I personally have found success with and most certainly not the only way. The playbooks/roles are intended to be working examples that you can use as or adjust/improve for your personal use cases.

Now that this has been said, let's get on with it.

Defining variables globally or per role

This topic may not seem important enough to review, but in reality with Ansible you have more options than usual. With that thought, you will have to decide on how you will define your variables within the roles.

Ansible has a variable definition hierarchy it follows. You have the option to define the value of a variable placed within your playbook/role globally, assigning it to a group of hosts or local to that specific role only. Defining the value globally would mean that all playbooks/roles could use that value and apply it to a group of hosts. Verses if you set the value locally to that role, the role will pick up the variables from here first.

Globally defined variables value would be defined within a file located in the `group_vars/` directory of the playbook. The filename would have to match a group name set in the `hosts` file. To recap this process, please refer to the Defining variable values section in `Chapter 2`, *Introduction to Ansible*. The advantage of this approach is you can set the variable value once and have your playbooks/roles just reuse the value. It simplifies defining variables overall and the task of updating the values as needed. The negative aspect to this approach is if you wish to reuse a variable name and want to provide a different value on a per role basis. This is where the alternative option comes into play.

Defining the variable value local to the role allows the reuse of a variable name and the capability to define different values for that variable. Through my experimentation of creating playbooks/roles against an OpenStack cloud, I have found defining the variables locally to the role seems to be the best option. My overall approach to creating roles is to create roles to be as simple as possible and to accomplish a single administrative task. Try not to combine multiple administrative tasks into a single role. Keeping the role simple enables the ability to reuse the role and keeps in line with Ansible's best practices.

So, the first framework decision we are making here is to define variable values locally to the role. Now we can move on to the next consideration/decision point, which is whether to use the OpenStack API or CLI to execute administrative commands.

OpenStack API or CLI?

Again, this decision may seem unimportant at a high level. Deciding to use the OpenStack API or CLI could drastically change the overall structure and approach to creating your playbooks/roles. In `Chapter 1`, *Introduction to OpenStack*, we covered the differences between the OpenStack API and CLI.

One thing that should have stood out is that the CLI is much easier to use and code against with Ansible. Keep in mind that the CLI still executes API commands behind the scenes dealing with all the token and JSON interpretation stuff for you. This allows zero loss in functionality.

The second framework decision we are declaring is to use the native OpenStack modules that come with Ansible when making calls to your OpenStack cloud. The only deviation from this decision would be to use CLI commands if there is not a module available to handle a task we need coded. With this decision, we have also chosen to use the `clouds.yaml` file mentioned in `Chapter 2`, *Introduction to Ansible* to store our credentials.

One last consideration now is to decide from where do we wish to execute the playbooks.

Where to run Ansible

My next statement may be a bit obvious, but the playbooks need to be executed from a workstation/server with Ansible installed. Now that we have this out of the way, let's explore our options:

- My first recommendation is not to run the playbooks directly from any of the OpenStack controller nodes. The controller nodes have plenty of work to do just to keep OpenStack going, no need to add additional burden.
- The other option is to execute the playbooks from some sort of centralized Ansible server in your environment. Although this is a totally viable option, I have a better one for you.

Since I am a huge fan and advocate for the **openstack-ansible** (**OSA**) method of deploying OpenStack, the playbooks/roles out of the box will use some of the great features offered with OSA. My last sentence may seem a bit off topic, but it will make more sense shortly.

One of the greatest features that come with running OSA is the built-in dynamic inventory script. This feature removes your burden of keeping inventory of your OpenStack service locations in a `hosts` file. In order to benefit from this feature, you would need to execute the playbooks/roles from the OSA deployment server. This in the big picture makes sense to keep all the Ansible playbooks/roles together (deployment and administration scripts).

The other compelling reason why this is the best option is that the OSA deployment server is already set up to communicate with the LXC containers where the OpenStack services are located. This point becomes very important when/if you want to make OpenStack service configuration changes with Ansible.

The last feature of OSA that I would like to highlight is the fact that it comes with a container designated just to administer your OpenStack cloud called the **utility** container. That container comes with every OpenStack service CLI package installed and ready to go. Yes, this is one less thing for you to worry about. This is one of the main reasons why I love me some OSA.

We now have our last framework decision, which is to execute the playbooks from the OSA deployment server in order to take full advantage of all the features OSA has to offer us (it just feels right). Now that we are all armed with a ton of good information and coding framework, all we have left is to create our first playbook and roles.

Coding the playbooks and roles

Before we start, we should first reflect back to the beginning of this chapter. We outlined the steps to create users and projects within your OpenStack cloud. Here, they are again for a quick reference:

- Creating the user (with a corresponding complex secure password)
- Creating the project for the user
- Linking that user to that project while assigning that user with the appropriate role

The first step to tackle is the user creation portion of the process. Creating the user is a simple task within OpenStack, so why not add some administration flare to go along with it. A part of the process of creating a user is assigning that user an appropriate password. We will include that as part of the role that creates the user and the project we will assign the user to.

When creating a playbook, I normally start with creating roles to handle the administrative tasks needed. The role will contain all the executable code against the OpenStack cloud. The playbook will contain the host to run the role against (in this case, it will be the utility container), the role(s) to execute, and other execution settings. The role to handle this administrative task will be named create-users-env.

The directory structure for our playbook will start off looking something like this:

```
base.yml              # master playbook for user creation
group_vars/
   util_container     # assign variable values for this host group
hosts                 # static host inventory file
roles/
   create-users-env   # user/project creation role
   tasks/
      main.yml        # tasks file for this role
   vars/
      main.yml        # variables associated with this role
```

Since we will start with the role task file assembly, let's create the `main.yml` file within the `create-users-env/tasks` directory. The initail contents of this file will look like this:

```
---

- name: Install random password generator package
  apt: name={{item}} state=present
  with_items:
   - apg

- name: Random generate passwords
  command: apg -n {{ pass_cnt }} -M NCL -q
  register: passwdss

- name: Create users
  os_user:
   cloud: "{{CLOUD_NAME}}"
   state: present
   name: "{{ item.0 }}"
   password: "{{ item.1 }}"
   domain: default
  with_together:
   - "{{userid}}"
   - "{{passwdss.stdout_lines}}"
```

Now we can walk through in more detail the three preceding tasks that were just added to the role. The very first following task sets the groundwork to use the `apg` package, which generates several random passwords:

```
- name: Install random password generator package
  apt: name={{item}} state=present
  with_items:
   - apg
```

Since in the second task we will use the `apg` package to generate passwords for us, we had to make sure that it was installed on the host executing the playbook/role. The `apt` module from Ansible is a very useful tool to manage Debian/Ubuntu packages. Defining the `{{item}}` parameter value with the module allows us to loop through multiple packages listed later inside the `with_items` statement. In this particular case, it is not needed since we are only installing one package, but at the same time does us no harm. Moving on to the second task:

```
- name: Random generate passwords
  command: apg -n {{ pass_cnt }} -M NCL -q
  register: passwdss
```

The second task now will execute the `apg` package using the command module from Ansible.

> The command module will be one of the mostly used modules when working with Ansible. It basically can handle executing any command/package with the exception of any commands that will use shell variables and shell-specific operations, such as: <, >, |, and &.

With the command module, we are passing the `apg` command with specific parameters `-n {{ pass_cnt }} -M NCL -q`. Most of the parameters are standard options for `apg` with the exception of the variable defined `{{ pass_cnt }}`. Setting this parameter allows us to adjust the number of passwords generated from the variable file set for this role (found in the `create-users-env/vars` directory). We will examine the variable file shortly. One of the last steps in this task is to register the output of the `apg` command into a variable named `passwdss`. This variable will be used later in this role.

The third task added to the role will now create the user within your OpenStack cloud. As seen here again, using the `os_user` module, we will execute the Keystone command to create a user with authentication parameters:

```
- name: Create users
  os_user:
   cloud: "{{CLOUD_NAME}}"
   state: present
   name: "{{ item.0 }}"
   password: "{{ item.1 }}"
   domain: default
  with_together:
   - "{{userid}}"
   - "{{passwdss.stdout_lines}}"
```

Within the task, we will also define a few variables to be used:

```
{{ item.0 }}  # variable placeholder used to set the usernames from the
list
               defined in the userid variable

{{ item.1 }}  # variable placeholder used to read in the output from the
apg
               command found within the passwdss variable registered
earlier
```

Placing variables within your commands sets you up to create roles with core code that you will not have to update every time it is used. It is a much simpler process to just update variable files instead of continuously altering role tasks.

The other special item part of this task is the use of the `with_together` Ansible loop command. This command allows us to loop through separate sets of variable values pairing them together in the defined order. Since the passwords are random, we do not care what user gets which password.

So now that we have our user creation code in the role, the next step is to create the user's project. The next two tasks are shown here:

```
- name: Create user environments
  os_project:
    cloud: "{{CLOUD_NAME}}"
    state: present
    name: "{{ item }}"
    description: "{{ item }}"
    domain_id: default
    enabled: True
  with_items: "{{tenantid}}"

- name: Assign user to specified role in designated environment
  os_user_role:
    cloud: "{{CLOUD_NAME}}"
    user: "{{ item.0 }}"
    role: "{{ urole }}"
    project: "{{ item.1 }}"
  with_together:
    - "{{userid}}"
    - "{{tenantid}}"
```

This first task will create the project with the `os-project` module. Project name and description will come from the `tenantid` variable. The next preceding task will then assign the user we created earlier to this newly created project with a role value set by the `urole` variable.

You will note that these tasks are very similar to the previous task used to create the user and also use similar Ansible parameters. As you can see, it will begin to form a repeated pattern. This really helps simply the code creation.

The last task part of the role will simply provide an output of the users created and their corresponding passwords. This step will give you (as the cloud operator) a very simple output with all the information you would need to save and/or pass on to the cloud consumer. Although this step is not required to complete the overall administrative task, it is nice. See the following task:

```
- name: User password assignment
  debug: msg="User {{ item.0 }} was added to {{ item.2 }} project, with the
assigned password of {{ item.1 }}"
  with_together:
    - userid
    - passwdss.stdout_lines
    - tenantid
```

In this task, we will use the debug module to show the output of the variable we set either manually or dynamically using the register Ansible command. The output will look something like this:

```
TASK: [create-users-env | User password assignment] *****************************
ok: [172.29.236.199] => (item=['mrkt-dev01', u'edribSov7', 'MRKT-Proj01']) => {
    "item": [
        "mrkt-dev01",
        "edribSov7",
        "MRKT-Proj01"
    ],
    "msg": "User mrkt-dev01 was added to MRKT-Proj01 tenant, with the assigned password of edribSov7"
}
ok: [172.29.236.199] => (item=['mrkt-dev02', u'wiawWef0', 'MRKT-Proj02']) => {
    "item": [
        "mrkt-dev02",
        "wiawWef0",
        "MRKT-Proj02"
    ],
    "msg": "User mrkt-dev02 was added to MRKT-Proj02 tenant, with the assigned password of wiawWef0"
}
ok: [172.29.236.199] => (item=['mrkt-dev03', u'PhiadCoup9', 'MRKT-Proj03']) => {
    "item": [
        "mrkt-dev03",
        "PhiadCoup9",
        "MRKT-Proj03"
    ],
    "msg": "User mrkt-dev03 was added to MRKT-Proj03 tenant, with the assigned password of PhiadCoup9"
}
ok: [172.29.236.199] => (item=['mrkt-dev04', u'0KnierAm4', 'MRKT-Proj04']) => {
    "item": [
        "mrkt-dev04",
        "0KnierAm4",
        "MRKT-Proj04"
    ],
    "msg": "User mrkt-dev04 was added to MRKT-Proj04 tenant, with the assigned password of 0KnierAm4"
}
ok: [172.29.236.199] => (item=['mrkt-dev05', u'Knyquits7', 'MRKT-Proj05']) => {
    "item": [
        "mrkt-dev05",
        "Knyquits7",
        "MRKT-Proj05"
    ],
    "msg": "User mrkt-dev05 was added to MRKT-Proj05 tenant, with the assigned password of Knyquits7"
}
```

Believe it or not, you have just created your very first OpenStack administration role. To support this role, we now need to create the variable file that will go along with it. The variable filename, `main.yml`, located in the `create-users-env/vars` directory, is very similar in structure to the task file.

Keep in mind that the values defined in the variable file are intended to be changed before each execution for normal every day use.

The values shown in the following example are just working examples. Let's take a look:

```
---
pass_cnt: 10
userid: [ 'mrkt-dev01', 'mrkt-dev02', 'mrkt-dev03', 'mrkt-dev04', 'mrkt-
dev05', 'mrkt-dev06', 'mrkt-dev07', 'mrkt-dev08', 'mrkt-dev09', 'mrkt-
dev10' ]
tenantid: [ 'MRKT-Proj01', 'MRKT-Proj02', 'MRKT-Proj03', 'MRKT-Proj04',
'MRKT-Proj05', 'MRKT-Proj06', 'MRKT-Proj07', 'MRKT-Proj08', 'MRKT-Proj09',
'MRKT-Proj10' ]
urole: _member_
```

Let's take a moment to break down each variable. The summary would be:

```
pass_cnt   # with the value of 10, we would be creating 10 random passwords
             with apg

userid     # the value is a comma delimited list of users to loop through
             when executing the user-create Keystone command

tenanted   # the value is a comma delimited list of tenant names to loop
             through when executing the tenant-create Keystone command

urole      # with the value of _member_, the user would be assigned the
             member role to the tenant created
```

This pretty much concludes what is involved in creating a variable file. We can now move on to the base of this playbook and create the master playbook file named `base.yml`, located in the `root` directory of the playbook directory. The contents of the `base.yml` file would be:

```
---
# This playbook used to demo OpenStack Juno user, role and project
features.

- hosts: util_container
  remote_user: root
```

```
    become: true
    roles:
create-users-env
```

The summary of this file is as follows:

```
hosts       # the host or host group to execute the playbook against

remote_user # the user to use when executing the playbook on the
              remote host(s)
become      # will tell Ansible to become the above user on the
              remote host(s)
 roles      # provide a list of roles to execute as part of
              this playbook
```

The last two areas of attention left before completing the playbook and making it ready for execution are creating the hosts inventory file and the global variable file. In this case, we are using a static host inventory file to keep things simple, but in future chapters, we will instead use the OSA dynamic inventory file. Because we are using the static inventory file, we will have to discover the name and/or IP address of the utility container.

This can be accomplished by running the following command on any of the controller nodes:

$ lxc-ls –fancy

Then, look for something similar to the highlighted item in the output:

```
root@021579-infra01:~# lxc-ls --fancy
NAME                                        STATE    IPV4                                          IPV6  AUTOSTART
-------------------------------------------------------------------------------------------------------------------
infra1_cinder_api_container-393b8b30        RUNNING  10.0.3.41, 172.29.236.235, 172.29.244.42   -     YES (onboot, rpc)
infra1_galera_container-d437bc41            RUNNING  10.0.3.116, 172.29.236.180                 -     YES (onboot, rpc)
infra1_glance_container-e03c5cd6            RUNNING  10.0.3.8, 172.29.236.164, 172.29.244.239   -     YES (onboot, rpc)
infra1_heat_apis_container-7a4707d8         RUNNING  10.0.3.27, 172.29.236.128                  -     YES (onboot, rpc)
infra1_heat_engine_container-789945f2       RUNNING  10.0.3.124, 172.29.236.250                 -     YES (onboot, rpc)
infra1_horizon_container-bf709bdd           RUNNING  10.0.3.226, 172.29.236.184                 -     YES (onboot, rpc)
infra1_keystone_container-422809c1          RUNNING  10.0.3.81, 172.29.236.39                   -     YES (onboot, rpc)
infra1_memcached_container-9f20fcd3         RUNNING  10.0.3.64, 172.29.236.42                   -     YES (onboot, rpc)
infra1_neutron_agents_container-1812d9f0    RUNNING  10.0.3.36, 172.29.236.67, 172.29.240.110   -     YES (onboot, rpc)
infra1_neutron_server_container-4626b33a    RUNNING  10.0.3.237, 172.29.236.24                  -     YES (onboot, rpc)
infra1_nova_api_ec2_container-e7a0d92c      RUNNING  10.0.3.165, 172.29.236.214                 -     YES (onboot, rpc)
infra1_nova_api_metadata_container-3284dcc5 RUNNING  10.0.3.23, 172.29.236.168                  -     YES (onboot, rpc)
infra1_nova_api_os_compute_container-448b89f1 RUNNING 10.0.3.143, 172.29.236.204                -     YES (onboot, rpc)
infra1_nova_cert_container-84a948f4         RUNNING  10.0.3.57, 172.29.236.92                   -     YES (onboot, rpc)
infra1_nova_conductor_container-df003a17    RUNNING  10.0.3.221, 172.29.236.134                 -     YES (onboot, rpc)
infra1_nova_scheduler_container-e6d32a0a    RUNNING  10.0.3.102, 172.29.236.28                  -     YES (onboot, rpc)
infra1_nova_spice_console_container-dd12200f RUNNING 10.0.3.62, 172.29.236.212                  -     YES (onboot, rpc)
infra1_rabbit_mq_container-5195a7b7         RUNNING  10.0.3.84, 172.29.236.231                  -     YES (onboot, rpc)
infra1_rsyslog_container-f422b60c           RUNNING  10.0.3.206, 172.29.236.52                  -     YES (onboot, rpc)
infra1_utility_container-c5589031           RUNNING  10.0.3.16, 172.29.236.199                  -     YES (onboot, rpc)
root@021579-infra01:~#
```

Then, add the utility container IP address to the hosts file as follows:

```
[localhost]
localhost ansible_connection=local

[util_container]
172.29.236.199
```

Last but not least, you then would create the global variable file inside the `group_vars/` directory. Remember that the file must be named to match the host or host group defined in the master playbook. Since we called the host group `util_container`, we must then name the variable file the exact same name. The contents of the `util_container` global variable file would be:

```
# Here are variables related globally to the util_container host group

CLOUD_NAME: default
```

ProTip

Always create/use an automation service account when executing commands against a system remotely. Never use the built-in admin and/or your personal account for that system. The use of service accounts makes for simple troubleshooting and system audits.

Guess what…you made it! We have just completely finished our very first OpenStack administration playbook and role. Let's finish up this chapter with a quick review of the playbook and role just created.

Reviewing playbooks and roles

To get right to it, we can start from the top with the role we created named `create-users-env`. The completed role and file named `main.yml` located in the `create-users-env/tasks` directory looks like this:

```
---

- name: Install random password generator package
  apt: name={{item}} state=present
  with_items:
    - apg

- name: Random generate passwords
  command: apg -n {{ pass_cnt }} -M NCL -q
  register: passwdss
```

```
 - name: Create users
  os_user:
   cloud: "{{CLOUD_NAME}}"
   state: present
   name: "{{ item.0 }}"
   password: "{{ item.1 }}"
   domain: default
  with_together:
   - "{{userid}}"
   - "{{passwdss.stdout_lines}}"

 - name: Create user environments
  os_project:
   cloud: "{{CLOUD_NAME}}"
   state: present
   name: "{{ item }}"
   description: "{{ item }}"
   domain_id: default
   enabled: True
  with_items: "{{tenantid}}"

 - name: Assign user to specified role in designated environment
  os_user_role:
   cloud: "{{CLOUD_NAME}}"
   user: "{{ item.0 }}"
   role: "{{ urole }}"
   project: "{{ item.1 }}"
  with_together:
   - "{{userid}}"
   - "{{tenantid}}"
 - name: User password assignment
  debug: msg="User {{ item.0 }} was added to {{ item.2 }} tenant, with the
assigned password of {{ item.1 }}"
  with_together:
   - userid
   - passwdss.stdout_lines
   - tenantid
```

The corresponding variable file named `main.yml`, located in the `create-users-env/vars` directory, for this role will look like this:

```
---
pass_cnt: 10
userid: [ 'mrkt-dev01', 'mrkt-dev02', 'mrkt-dev03', 'mrkt-dev04', 'mrkt-
dev05', 'mrkt-dev06', 'mrkt-dev07', 'mrkt-dev08', 'mrkt-dev09', 'mrkt-
dev10' ]
tenantid: [ 'MRKT-Proj01', 'MRKT-Proj02', 'MRKT-Proj03', 'MRKT-Proj04',
'MRKT-Proj05', 'MRKT-Proj06', 'MRKT-Proj07', 'MRKT-Proj08', 'MRKT-Proj09',
```

```
'MRKT-Proj10' ]
urole: _member_
```

Next, the master playbook file named `base.yml`, located in the `root` directory of the playbook directory, will look like this:

```
---
# This playbook used to demo OpenStack Juno user, role and project
features.

- hosts: util_container
  remote_user: root
  become: true
  roles:
    create-users-env
```

Following that we created the `hosts` file, which also is located in the `root` directory of the `playbook` directory.

```
[localhost]
localhost ansible_connection=local

[util_container]
172.29.236.199
```

Finally, we wrapped this playbook all up by creating the global variable file named `util_container`, saving it to the `group_vars/` directory of the `playbook` directory:

```
# Here are variables related globally to the util_container host group

CLOUD_NAME: default
```

As promised earlier, I felt that it was very important to provide the fully working Ansible playbooks and roles for your consumption. You can use them as is and/or as a springboard to creating new/improved Ansible code. The code can be found in the GitHub repository, `https://github.com/os-admin-with-ansible/os-admin-with-ansible-v2`.

Now of course, we have to test out our work. Assuming that you have cloned the GitHub repository mentioned earlier, the command to test out the playbook from the Deployment node would be as follows:

```
$ cd os-admin-with-ansible-v2
$ ansible-playbook -i hosts base.yml
```

Summary

See now that was not so bad, right? Ansible really does a great job in streamlining the effort involved in automating OpenStack administrative tasks. You can now reuse that role over and over again, cutting the amount of time creating users and projects down to single digit minutes. The time investment is well worth the benefits.

In this chapter, we created users and projects within OpenStack via the API and CLI. We gathered an understanding of basic automation considerations. We also developed Ansible playbooks and roles to automate the user and project creation.

With this great foundation, we are ready to move on to our next administrative task of customizing your clouds quotas. The next chapter will include a general understanding of what quotas are and how they are used within your OpenStack cloud. We will then transition to the exercise of creating quotas manually and then concluding with how to automate that task with Ansible. See you in `Chapter 4`, *Customizing Your Clouds Quotas*!

4
Customizing Your Clouds Quotas

Now that we have tackled creating our first OpenStack administration playbook, it is time to progress onto our next task. The next task we will cover is how to customize the project quotas in your cloud. This is normally the next step in the process of setting up new projects/tenants for your cloud consumers. We will step through how one would manually do this first and then transition into creating a playbook with roles to fully automate it:

- Defining and creating quotas
- Automation considerations
- Coding the playbook and roles
- Playbook and role review

Defining and creating quotas

What are quotas? Within OpenStack, you can set quotas on a tenant/project or user level in order to restrict the resource consumption allowed. The Compute service (Nova) manages the quota values and also enforces them. As a cloud operator, this is another important feature OpenStack offers. Quotas allow you to control the cloud's overall system capacity. You may ask, why not just set up one default quota and let every project use it? We will step through why this approach may or may not work based on the particular use case. It is also worth mentioning that the Block Storage service (Cinder) also has the capability of setting quotas.

Since we now know that you can set quotas, let's review what resources can be restricted and what the default values are. The following table describes the type of quotas that can be set:

Quota Name	Defines the number of
Instances	Instances allowed in each project
Cores	Instance cores allowed in each project
RAM (MB)	RAM megabytes allowed in each instance
Floating IPs	Floating IPs allowed in each project
Fixed IPs	Fixed IPs allowed in each project
Metadata Items	Metadata items allowed in each instance
Injected Files	Injected files allowed in each project
Injected File Content Bytes	Content bytes allowed in each injected file
Keypairs	Keypairs allowed in each project
Security Groups	Security groups allowed in each project
Security Group Rules	Rules allowed in each security group
Server Groups	Server groups allowed in each project
Server Group Members	Server group members allowed in each project

As you can see, there are quite a few options to apply restrictions to. As a cloud operator, you would want to take full advantage of tuning these options on a per-project basis. Taking on this approach allows you to optimize your cloud usage, in essence stretching your resources further while provisioning only what is needed. As an administrator, I hated seeing wasted resources hanging out there when, if better controls were in place, they could be used for something else. Quotas serve as the opposite approach, also the concept of keeping the Cloud Consumer from exhausting all of the cloud resources.

Yes, the process of tuning quotas does involve efforts (aka extra work). Thus, the concept of setting global default quota values has become popular. To view the default quota values, you would execute the following command:

```
$ openstack --os-cloud=<cloud name> quota show <project name>
```

The output will look like this:

```
root@allinone-utility-container-fdb175b5:~# openstack --os-cloud=default quota show admin
+----------------------------+----------------------------------------------+
| Field                      | Value                                        |
+----------------------------+----------------------------------------------+
| backup_gigabytes           | 1000                                         |
| backups                    | 10                                           |
| cores                      | 20                                           |
| fixed-ips                  | -1                                           |
| floating-ips               | 50                                           |
| gigabytes                  | 1000                                         |
| gigabytes_lvm              | -1                                           |
| healthmonitor              | -1                                           |
| injected-file-size         | 10240                                        |
| injected-files             | 5                                            |
| injected-path-size         | 255                                          |
| instances                  | 10                                           |
| key-pairs                  | 100                                          |
| l7policy                   | -1                                           |
| listener                   | -1                                           |
| loadbalancer               | 10                                           |
| network                    | 10                                           |
| per_volume_gigabytes       | -1                                           |
| pool                       | 10                                           |
| port                       | 50                                           |
| project                    | 5408dd3366e943b694cae90a04d71c88             |
| properties                 | 128                                          |
| ram                        | 51200                                        |
| rbac_policy                | 10                                           |
| router                     | 10                                           |
| secgroup-rules             | 100                                          |
| secgroups                  | 10                                           |
| server_group_members       | 10                                           |
```

Whenever you wish to set a quota value to be unlimited, set the value to -1. This tells Nova to allow that resource to be unrestricted for that project or globally if set as default.

Now, let's focus on how we can adjust the quota values manually using CLI. For simplicity purposes, we will demonstrate the manual commands using the OpenStack CLI only.

Manually creating quotas

To be accurate, you only have the capability to update the values set for global quotas or quotas set for a specific tenant/project. You cannot create new quotas; just update the values. To list, update, and reset a quota involves sending requests to the Compute service (Nova).

Just like with every OpenStack service, you must authenticate first by sourcing the OpenRC file discussed in `Chapter 1`, *Introduction to OpenStack*. You would then need to provide the values for the quota you wish to update (refer to the table mentioned earlier for your options). Now, let's look at the following example:

```
$ source openrc
$ openstack quota set <project name> --instances=<value>
  --cores=<value>
```

Once the command is executed, no output is written back to the screen. You can then execute the `quota show` command to confirm the update.

A real life working example could look something like this:

```
$ openstack quota show admin
```

Keep in mind that the preceding example only shows updating the `instance` and `core` quotas for a project. There are other quota values that can be updated.

Setting up default quotas

In the event you wish to only set up a default quota that all tenant/projects and users will be assigned, the process is a bit different. Nova also manages the default quota assignments. Setting up a default quota can be very useful when you wish to quickly create a tenant/project or user with automatic built-in controls in place.

Nothing is worse than creating a project that has no resource restrictions by mistake, and before you know it, the consumers of that project have exhausted your cloud. Cloud is intended to give the consumers the impression of being limitless. In reality, we all know that there is no such thing; everything has a limit in some manner. From my experience, if you give a user 20 vCPU, they will use it all if allowed. Putting cloud resource restrictions in place is very important as a cloud operator.

The command to update the default quota for your cloud is given later. This command can be executed after authenticating just as in the previous examples. The quota options are the same as updating a project or user-specific quota. Again, please refer to the table mentioned earlier for your options. Here is an example:

```
$ openstack quota set <quota class name> --ram=<value>
  --security-groups=<value>
```

One of the main differences with the preceding command is you must supply something that Nova refers to as `quota` class. A `quota` class is the way Nova distinguishes between a default `quota` and a custom `quota` you may set up. Assuming future releases of Nova will include the ability to create additional `quota` classes. For now, you only have the ability to update the only `quota` class available, which is named `default`.

A working example of the command would look like this:

```
$ openstack quota set default --ram=-1 --security-groups=30
```

Please keep in mind, whatever you set the default `quota` values to is what every project or user will have configured initially.

Resetting quota values

A time may come when you may want to start fresh and reset a quota set for a project(s) or user(s). Fortunately, this is an easy process within OpenStack. You would use the `quota-delete` command for Nova. This will delete the custom quota and reset it back to the default quota. See the following example:

```
$ nova quota-delete --tenant=<tenant-id> [--user=<user-id>]
```

With the preceding command, you would supply either the tenant ID or the user ID to which you want to revert the quota back to the default values.

Automation considerations

When creating this role, there was only one automation decision that I had to make outside of the ones we covered in the previous chapter. All the other considerations carried over.

Because the Nova `quota` commands allow numerous options to be passed with no interdependencies, we have to figure out a way to not restrict that flexibility in the role and at the same time not require constant updates directly to the role. Ansible makes such a decision really easy by allowing variables to be passed as a `hash`. Within the variable file, you can then define the options for each project or user and have the task cycle through each project/user with those options.

I promise this is the last time I will make this disclaimer, but I felt that it is important to emphasize:

> There are many ways to approach automating tasks for OpenStack with Ansible, the ones shown in this book is just one way I personally have found success with and most certainly not the only way. The playbooks/roles are intended to be working examples you can use as is or adjust/improve for your personal use cases.

Just like last time, now that this has been said let's get on with creating this role.

Coding the playbooks and roles

We will now create a role that allows us to update a single and/or multiple project(s) quotas at one time. Updating a quota is a relatively simple two-step process. Step 1 is to record the tenant ID or user ID in which you wish to update the quota for. Then, step 2 is to actually update the quota.

Since we are only creating a role in this example, we can start with the `main.yml` file within the role directory named `adjust-quotas/tasks`. The contents at the beginning of this file will look like this:

```
---

- name: Adjust tenant quotas
  command: openstack --os-cloud="{{ CLOUD_NAME }}"
        quota set "{{ item.1 }}" "{{ item.0 }}"
  with_together:
   - "{{qoptions}}"
   - "{{tenantname}}"
```

Just like the manual commands we reviewed earlier in this chapter, you must supply the quota options you wish to adjust and the tenant name from the variable file we will review later. Again, we are using the `with_together` command to loop through the two variables defined pairing the values together.

Here is a further breakdown of the variables defined in the task:

```
{{ item.0 }}  # variable placeholder used to set the quota options to
update

{{ item.1 }}  # variable placeholder used to set the project name
```

When the role is executed, no output is generated in this particular case. If you wanted to provide an output to confirm the successful execution of the task, you can add the `quota show` command as an additional task in your role. An example of that would look like this:

```
- name: Confirm tenant quota update
  command: openstack --os-cloud="{{ CLOUD_NAME }}"
       quota show "{{ item.0 }}"
  with_items: "{{tenantname}}"
```

You have now completed your second OpenStack administration role. To support this role, we now need to create the variable file that will go along with it. The variable file named `main.yml`, which will be located in the `adjust-quotas/vars` directory.

Keep in mind that the values defined in the variable file are intended to be changed before each execution for normal everyday use.

The values shown in the following example are just working examples. Let's take a look:

```
---
qoptions: [ '--cores 30', '--instances 20', '--cores 20', '--instances 20',
'--cores 20' ]
tenantname: [ 'MRKT-Proj01', 'MRKT-Proj02', 'MRKT-Proj02', 'MRKT-Proj03',
'MRKT-Proj03' ]
```

Let's take a moment to break down each variable. The summary would be:

```
qoptions   # this is where you declare the quota options you wish to update,
each
           set of options and values are encapsulated within single quotes
           comma delimited; there is no limit on the number of options
that can
           be added
 tenantname # the value is a comma delimited list of tenant names you wish
           to update quotas for
```

Now that our variable file is created, we can move on to creating the master playbook file. Just like in the previous chapter, the file will be named `quota-update.yml` and saved to the root of the playbook directory. The contents of the `quota-update.yml` file would be:

```
---
# This playbook used to demo OpenStack Juno quota updates.

- hosts: util_container
  remote_user: root
  become: true
  roles:
adjust-quotas
```

The summary of this file is as follows:

```
hosts        # the host or host group to execute the playbook against

remote_user # the user to use when executing the playbook on the remote
host(s)

become       # will tell Ansible to become the above user on the remote
host(s)

roles        # provide a list of roles to execute as part of this playbook
```

All that is left is to populate our host inventory file and the global variable file. Since we already created these in the previous chapter, there is no need to repeat this process. The values defined earlier would remain the same. Here is a quick recap of how those files are configured.

Hosts file in the root of the playbook directory is:

```
[localhost]
localhost ansible_connection=local

[util_container]
172.29.236.199
```

Global variable file inside the `group_vars/` directory is:

```
# Here are variables related globally to the util_container host group

CLOUD_NAME: default
```

OK, so here we are, two administration playbooks and roles completed now. As always, we will finish up the chapter with a quick review of the playbook and role just created.

Reviewing playbooks and roles

To get right to it, we can start from the top with the role we created named `create-users-env`. The completed role and file, named `main.yml`, located in the `adjust-quotas/tasks` directory, looks like this:

```
---

- name: Adjust tenant quotas
  command: openstack --os-cloud="{{ CLOUD_NAME }}"
       quota set "{{ item.1 }}" "{{ item.0 }}"
  with_together:
   - "{{qoptions}}"
   - "{{tenantname}}"
```

The corresponding variable file, named `main.yml`, located in the `adjust-quota/vars` directory, for this role will look like this:

```
---
qoptions: [ '--cores 30', '--instances 20', '--cores 20', '--instances 20',
'--cores 20' ]
tenantname: [ 'MRKT-Proj01', 'MRKT-Proj02', 'MRKT-Proj02', 'MRKT-Proj03',
'MRKT-Proj03' ]
```

Next, the master playbook file, named `quota-update.yml`, located in the `root` of the `playbook` directory, will look like this:

```
---
# This playbook used to demo OpenStack Juno quota updates.

- hosts: util_container
  remote_user: root
  become: true
  roles:
  adjust-quotas
```

Following this, we created the hosts file, which also is located in the `root` directory of the `playbook` directory:

```
[localhost]
localhost ansible_connection=local

[util_container]
172.29.236.199
```

Finally, we wrapped this playbook all up by creating the global variable file named `util_container`, saving it to the `group_vars/` directory of the playbook:

```
# Here are variables related globally to the util_container host group

CLOUD_NAME: default
```

 The complete set of code can again be found in the following GitHub repository at `https://github.com/os-admin-with-ansible/os-admin-with-ansible-v2`.

Now of course, we have to test out our work. Assuming that you have cloned the GitHub repository mentioned earlier, the command to test out the playbook from the Deployment node would be as follows:

```
$ cd os-admin-with-ansible-v2
$ ansible-playbook -i hosts quota-update.yml
```

Summary

As an OpenStack operator quotas will be a focus on yours, so any effort in being able to streamlet that process will be beneficial. Ansible is the key to being able to simplify repeated tasks such as this. Just as in the previous chapter, you can use this role in combination with others as many times as you want. This is why, you want to design your roles to be the base generic task as much as possible .

Some of the things we covered in this chapter are defining what a quota within OpenStack is. We then took that knowledge and learned how to update a quota for a project/user using the OpenStack CLI. We applied some base principles as to why you would use the default cloud quotas and how to update them appropriately. Next, we reviewed how to reset any of the custom quotas created. Finally, we developed our very own Ansible playbook and role to automate updating custom project/user quotas.

Let's now to move on to the next chapter where we will take on the administrative task of snapshotting your cloud. The functionality of taking instance snapshots is a powerful tool if you wanted to use that instance as a gold copy and/or retain a backup of the instance. Understanding how to handle this sort of task on a cloud operator level is very beneficial. The next chapter will cover how to create snapshots manually, cover the power of being able to snapshot all instances within a project at once and then of course conclude with how to automate that task with Ansible. On to `Chapter 5`, *Snapshot Your Cloud*, we go!

5
Snapshot Your Cloud

In this chapter, we will cover the task of creating instance backups and/or snapshots using the native OpenStack capability built into the Compute service (Nova). When adopting a true cloud approach, the approach of scaling horizontally and disposable resources, you will find great use in leveraging snapshots versus traditional backups. Despite that it is good, the best practice is to understand both the capabilities and the proper use case for each. We will step through how to manually create backups or snapshots first and then transition to creating a playbook with roles to fully automate it on a tenant level. We will cover the following topics in this chapter:

- Defining backups and snapshots
- Manually creating backups and snapshots
- Restoring an instance backup
- Automation considerations
- Coding the playbook and roles
- The review of playbook and role

Defining backups and snapshots

From an OpenStack perspective, there are distinct differences between a backup and snapshot of an instance. Those differences could influence the use of each of those functions. Keep in mind that with keeping with true cloud behavior, all cloud resources are meant to be disposable. You may ask what that statement really means. It simply means that any instances or volumes (resources) created to support your application functions should be able to be recreated in some sort of automated fashion. Instilling the *pets versus cattle* analogy. No longer are the days of attempting to bring a sick VM back to life.

Destroy the instance, recreate it, and off you go again. These principles remove the want for instance backups. With this said, there will be cases where you may want to have a backup of an instance. So, let's first examine the capability of taking an instance backup.

The OpenStack Compute service (Nova) functionality of backing up an instance behaves just like any traditional backup process. A purpose of taking a backup of an instance would be to preserve the instances current state for later possible recovery. Just like any other back process; you can determine the type of backup and rotation schedule. Some possible `backup` type parameters can be **daily** or **weekly**. The rotation schedule would represent the number of backups to keep. A working example of the instance `backup` command via the Nova CLI would be as follows:

```
$ nova backup <instance><backup name><backup-type><rotation>
$ nova backup testinst bck-testinst weekly 5
```

In full transparency, the Nova `backup` functionality is not in a fully operational state as of the time this book was written. The `backup` command at this point in time is just a hook put into Nova to set up for future OpenStack service(s) focused solely on data protection. The OpenStack Data Protection service, code name **Raksha**, will be responsible for helping automate data protection tasks such as backups. Raksha is still under development, and it will appear in an upcoming OpenStack release. You can read more about Raksha at `https://wiki.openstack.org/wiki/Raksha`.

Now we can move on to talking about snapshots. The Nova functionality of taking a snapshot of an instance is similar to a backup, but instead of keeping the backup for recovery purposes, it is stored by the image service (Glance) as an image template. That image template can then be used to create additional instances just like the instance the original snapshot was taken from. It is like making a rubber stamp copy of the instance.

Please keep in mind that taking a traditional snapshot of an instance will temporarily pause the instance until the process completes. If you are seeking to take a snapshot without pausing the instance, please review the *Live Snapshots* capability details found at `http://docs.openstack.org/openstack-ops/content/snapshots.html`.

I often like the snapshot process to making a golden or gold image of a server that would be used to build additional servers. The steps taken would be exactly the same. Create the instance with the required OS, install necessary software packages, make suggested OS and application security tweaks, certify the applications functionality, and then create the snapshot. Having the snapshot capability at your fingertips without needing any third-party software is indeed yet another powerful tool OpenStack offers.

A working example of the instance snapshot command via the OpenStackClient CLI would be as follows:

```
$ openstack server image create
  --name=<snapshot name> <instance>
$ openstack server image create
  --name=snp-testinst testinst
```

Hopefully, this helped provide clear definitions around the differences between instance backups and snapshots. Let us now examine the steps required to manually create them using the CLI.

 For simplicity purposes, we will demonstrate the manual commands using the OpenStack CLI only.

Manually creating backups and snapshots

As stated earlier, the Compute service (Nova) handles the task of creating instance backups and snapshots. Just like with every OpenStack service, you must authenticate first either by sourcing the OpenRC file discussed in `Chapter 1`, *Introduction to OpenStack* or by passing authentication parameters in-line with the command. The two tasks individually require different parameter values to be provided in order to successfully execute the command. See the examples given later.

Here is an instance `backup` using the OpenRC file:

```
$ source openrc
$ nova backup <instance> <backup name>
  <backup-type><rotation>
```

Here is an instance `backup` passing authentication parameters in-line:

```
$ nova --os-username=<OS_USERNAME> --os-password=
  <OS_PASSWORD> --os-tenant-
  name=<OS_TENANT_NAME> --os-auth-url=<OS_AUTH_URL>
```

```
backup <instance><backup name>
<backup-type><rotation>
```

Once the command is executed, no output is written back to the screen. You can then execute the `openstack image show` command to confirm the update.

A real life working example with an OpenRC file could look something like this:

```
$ source openrc
$ openstack server list
$ nova backup vm-with-vol-my_instance-v35vvbw67u7s
  bck-vm-with-vol-my_instance-v35vvbw67u7s weekly 3
```

The output of the `openstack image list` command would then be:

```
root@allinone-utility-container-fdb175b5:~# openstack image list
+--------------------------------------+------------------------------------------+--------+
| ID                                   | Name                                     | Status |
+--------------------------------------+------------------------------------------+--------+
| 53bc650f-bf84-41f7-8125-38044a8df16a | bck-vm-with-vol-my_instance-v35vvbw67u7s | queued |
| ac03be00-46fd-4e5a-a00d-b75b34909e80 | ubuntu-server-14.04                      | active |
| 6684769b-c669-4ba8-8e53-b63f07962738 | cirros-0.3.3                             | active |
+--------------------------------------+------------------------------------------+--------+
root@allinone-utility-container-fdb175b5:~#
```

With the earlier-mentioned command, you can supply the instance ID or name. The example just shown uses the instance name. After sourcing the OpenRC file, the `openstack server list` command was executed in order to take note of the instance ID or name that you wish to backup. Once you have that information, the `nova backup` command can then be executed.

 The image service, code name Glance, is responsible for keeping inventory of backups, snapshots, and any images manually uploaded by the Cloud operator. To view the available inventory, you will have to issue Glance CLI commands and/or view them via the **Horizon** dashboard under the **Images** tab.

Here is an instance snapshot using an OpenRC file:

```
$ source openrc
$ openstack server image create
  --name=<snapshot name> <instance>
```

The following is an instance snapshot passing authentication parameters in-line:

```
$ openstack --os-cloud=default server image create
  --name=<snapshot name> <instance>
```

Once the command is executed, no output is written back to the screen. You can then execute the `openstack image list` command to confirm the update.

A real life working example with an OpenRC file could look something like this:

```
$ source openrc
$ openstack server list
$ openstack server image create --name=snap-vm-
  with-vol-my_instance-v35vvbw67u7s
  vm-with-vol-my_instance-v35vvbw67u7s
```

The output of the `openstack image list` command would then be:

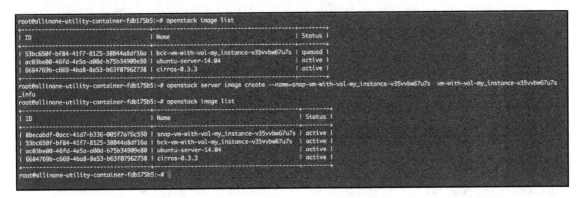

Now that we have covered how to create the instance backups and snapshots, it only felt right to demonstrate how you can then use them. Particularly, I would like to focus on using the instance backups, since I noticed a severe lack of documentation around this functionality.

Restoring an instance backup

Although the instance `backup` functionality is not 100% active from a scheduled job/automation perspective, you can still use instance backups to restore an instance back to a particular point in time. In order to do this, you would use the `nova rebuild` command within the Nova CLI. This command will signal the instance to shut down, re-image the instance using the `backup` file referenced and then reboot the instance.

A working example of the `nova rebuild` command via the Nova CLI would be as follows:

```
$ nova rebuild <instance> <image name>
$ nova rebuild vm-with-vol-my_instance-v35vvbw67u7s
  snap-vm-with-vol-my_instance-v35vvbw67u7s
```

The `nova rebuild` command also has quite a few optional arguments that can be passed with the command. Those optional arguments can do things such as reset the admin password or change the name of the instance, for example. I would suggest taking a look at the OpenStack CLI documentation, which can be found at `http://docs.openstack.org/cli-reference/content/novaclient_commands.html#novaclient_subcommand_rebuild`.

Automation considerations

Automating this task was pretty straightforward and did not require any new framework decisions. All the other automation decisions we reviewed were previously carried over.

There was one area worth highlighting that you may too face when automating OpenStack tasks using the CLI. The default output of the CLI is **pretty-printed** (using the Python **prettytable** module) of which at times is not so pretty when you want to sort through the output. Some CLI commands allow specific formatting, but in the event the command does not allow it, you have other options. This is where the `awk` command becomes your very close ally again. In the next section, you will note the specific use of the `awk` command to filter out the values we need for the next task within the role.

It feels like we are ready to proceed now with creating our next playbook and role.

Coding the playbooks and roles

The playbook and role we will now create will allow you to take a snapshot of all instances within a single tenant at one time. This distinct task was chosen to try to keep the role simple and not to overcomplicate the tasks. You could very well also create a role to snapshot or backup all instances in all tenants with the removal of just one parameter. Pretty awesome, right? Well, send your thank you cards to Ansible for that.

At the beginning of this chapter, we reviewed the process of how to take instance backups and snapshots. It was a simple two-step process. For the purposes of automating this task, we have to add an additional step to the process. That step would be to get the tenant ID for the tenant we plan to take the snapshot(s) from. So in the big picture, there would be three steps. *Step 1* is to record the tenant ID in which you wish to take instance snapshot(s) for. *Step 2* is to now list all instance IDs from the tenant. Then, finally, *Step 3* is to actually take the instance snapshot(s).

Since we are only creating a role in this example, we can start by the main.yml file within the role directory named create-snapshot/tasks. The beginning contents of this file will look like this:

```
    ---

    - name: Retrieve tenantID
      shell: openstack --os-cloud="{{ CLOUD_NAME }}"
          project list | awk '/ "{{tenantname}}" / { print $2 }'
      register: tenantid
```

The first step of pulling the tenant ID is straightforward with the use of the awk command and pipe (|) symbol. This approach is something you will see in a lot of the OpenStack documentation. It allows you to take the output of one command and filter out the parts you want to keep. First, we will execute the project list command, that output will then be used with a filter, the filter will search for the tenant name provided via the variable named tenantname, and finally, output the second column value from the original project list command. That final output will then be registered with the variable named tenantid. The tenantname variable is defined the same way as in the previous chapter.

Remember that the shell module is used here because we are executing commands that require shell-specific operations.

The next task will now list out all instance IDs from the tenant. The code to accomplish this looks like this:

```
    - name: Retrieve instance id from tenant
      shell: openstack --os-cloud="{{ CLOUD_NAME }}"
          server list --all-projects --project "{{ tenantid.stdout }}" | awk 'NR
    > 3 { print $2 }'
      register: instid
```

This task is very similar to the first one, except the fact that we are using the OpenStackClient CLI instead to list the instances and filtering out just IDs removing all leading or trailing characters. I found that the `openstack server list` command when using Ansible was very specific about how the instance ID/name had to be provided. In order to accomplish this, I decided to use one of the `awk` command's built-in variables named `NR`.

The `NR` variable (number of records) within `awk` is intended to supply you with the number of records or the line number of the content being filtered. In turn, the `NR` variable can be used to focus examination on certain lines as well. Here, we use the variable to skip the first three lines of the CLI output. This example shows what the normal output would be:

```
root@allinone-utility-container-fdb175b5:~# openstack server list --all-projects
+--------------------------------------+-----------------------------------------+--------+------------------------------+
| ID                                   | Name                                    | Status | Networks                     |
+--------------------------------------+-----------------------------------------+--------+------------------------------+
| a6a1cbaa-3c17-4aac-9fd1-3ffe8c7781a6 | vm-with-vol-my_instance-v35vvbw67u7s    | ACTIVE | private-network=10.1.100.37  |
+--------------------------------------+-----------------------------------------+--------+------------------------------+
root@allinone-utility-container-fdb175b5:~#
```

Then, here is what the output looks like when adding the `awk` command, `awk 'NR > 3 { print $2 }'`:

```
root@allinone-utility-container-fdb175b5:~# openstack server list --all-projects
+--------------------------------------+-----------------------------------------+--------+------------------------------+
| ID                                   | Name                                    | Status | Networks                     |
+--------------------------------------+-----------------------------------------+--------+------------------------------+
| a6a1cbaa-3c17-4aac-9fd1-3ffe8c7781a6 | vm-with-vol-my_instance-v35vvbw67u7s    | ACTIVE | private-network=10.1.100.37  |
+--------------------------------------+-----------------------------------------+--------+------------------------------+
root@allinone-utility-container-fdb175b5:~# openstack server list --all-projects | awk 'NR > 3 { print $2 }'
a6a1cbaa-3c17-4aac-9fd1-3ffe8c7781a6

root@allinone-utility-container-fdb175b5:~#
```

Finally, now that we have our list of instances, we can conclude with the last task of taking the snapshot(s). The code to do this would look like this:

```
- name: Create instance snapshot
  command: openstack --os-cloud="{{ CLOUD_NAME }}"
     server image create --name="{{ tenantname }}"-snap-"{{ item }}" "{{
  item }}"
  with_items: "{{instid.stdout_lines}}"
  register: command_result
  failed_when: "'_info' not in command_result.stderr"
```

Just as in the previous chapter, defining the {{item}} parameter value with the module allows us to loop through multiple packages listed here inside the with_items statement. Also, remember that getting the output after registering values into a variable within Ansible requires you to query the stdout or stdout_lines section of the JSON data structure. We then repurposed the tenant name and instance ID to name the snapshot for easy future reference. The snapshot name itself can be anything you desire, I just felt this naming convention made the most sense.

The last two lines in the preceding code, register and failed_when, had to be added due to the output of the openstack server image create command. If you wanted to provide an output to confirm the successful execution of the task, you can add the openstack image list command as an additional task in your role and either have the task output printed to the screen or saved in a file. An example of printing the output to the screen would look like this:

```
- name: Confirm instance snapshot(s)
  shell: openstack --os-cloud="{{ CLOUD_NAME }}"
      image list --format value --column Name
  register: snapchk

- name: Image list output
  debug: msg="{{ item }}"
  with_items: "{{snapchk.stdout_lines}}"
```

You have now completed your third OpenStack administration role. To support this role, we now need to create the variable file that will go along with it. The variable file named main.yml will be located in the create-snapshot/vars directory.

 Keep in mind that the values defined in the variable file are intended to be changed before each execution for normal everyday use.

For this role, there was the only variable that was needed:

```
---
tenantname: MRKT-Proj01
```

This variable is intended to be a single value of one of the tenant names for which the instance snapshot(s) will be taken.

Now that our variable file is created, we can move on to creating the master playbook file. The file will be named snapshot-tenant.yml and saved to the root directory of the playbook directory.

The playbook and role names can be anything you choose. Specific names have been provided here in order to allow you to easily follow along and reference the completed code found in the GitHub repository. The only warning is whatever you decide to name the roles must remain uniform when referenced from within the playbook(s).

The contents of the `snapshot-tenant.yml` file would be:

```
---
# This playbook used to demo OpenStack Newton user, role, image and volume
features.

- hosts: util_container
  remote_user: root
  become: true
  roles:
    - create-snapshot
```

The summary of this file is as follows:

```
hosts        # the host or host group to execute the playbook against

remote_user # the user to use when executing the playbook on the remote
host(s)

become       # will tell Ansible to become the above user on the remote
host(s)

roles        # provide a list of roles to execute as part of this playbook
```

All that is left is to populate our host `inventory` file and the global `variable` file. Since we already created these in the previous chapter, there is no need to repeat this process. The values defined earlier would remain the same. Here is a quick recap of how those files are configured.

The `hosts` file in the `root` directory of the playbook directory is:

```
[localhost]
localhost ansible_connection=local

[util_container]
172.29.236.199
```

A global variable file inside the `group_vars/` directory is:

```
# Here are variables related globally to the util_container host group

CLOUD_NAME: default
```

Great job in completing your third administration playbook and role! As always, we will finish up the chapter with a quick review of the playbook and role just created.

Reviewing playbooks and roles

Let's jump right into examining the role we created, named `create-snapshot`. The completed role and file, named `main.yml`, located in the `create-snapshot/tasks` directory, looks like this:

```
---

- name: Retrieve tenantID
  shell: openstack --os-cloud="{{ CLOUD_NAME }}"
      project list | awk '/ "{{tenantname}}" / { print $2 }'
  register: tenantid

- name: Retrieve instance id from tenant
  shell: openstack --os-cloud="{{ CLOUD_NAME }}"
      server list --all-projects --project "{{ tenantid.stdout }}" | awk 'NR
> 3 { print $2 }'
  register: instid

- name: Create instance snapshot
  command: openstack --os-cloud="{{ CLOUD_NAME }}"
      server image create --name="{{ tenantname }}"-snap-"{{ item }}" "{{
item }}"
  with_items: "{{instid.stdout_lines}}"
  register: command_result
  failed_when: "'_info' not in command_result.stderr"
```

The corresponding variable file, named `main.yml`, located in the `create-snapshot/vars` directory, for this role will look like this:

```
---
tenantname: MRKT-Proj01
```

Next, the master playbook file, named `snapshot-tenant.yml`, located in the `root` directory of the playbook directory, will look like this:

```
---
# This playbook used to demo OpenStack Newton user, role, image and volume
features.

- hosts: util_container
  remote_user: root
  become: true
  roles:
    - create-snapshot
```

Following this we created the `hosts` file, which also is located in the `root` directory of the `playbook` directory:

```
[localhost]
localhost ansible_connection=local

[util_container]
172.29.236.199
```

Finally, creating the global variable file, named `util_container`, and saving it to the `group_vars/` directory of the playbook would complete the playbook:

```
# Here are variables related globally to the util_container host group

CLOUD_NAME: default
```

The complete set of code can again be found in the GitHub repository at `https://github.com/os-admin-with-ansible/os-admin-with-ansible-v2`.

We cannot finish up this chapter without first testing out our work. Assuming that you have cloned the preceding GitHub repository, the command to test out the playbook from the Deployment node would be as follows:

```
$ cd os-admin-with-ansible-v2
$ ansible-playbook -i hosts snapshot-tenant.yml
```

Summary

Once you get started creating playbooks and roles with Ansible, you will find that you are able to reuse a lot of code for many different purposes. In this chapter, we were able to create another role very similar to the previous chapter, but include a totally different task very quickly and easily. Always remember to design your roles to be the base generic task as much as possible. I sincerely cannot emphasize that tip enough. It could be the difference of taking minutes/hours versus days to automate something.

In this chapter, we defined and described the difference between instance backups and snapshots. We explained the process, how to manually create backups and snapshots using the OpenStack CLI. We also reviewed an example of how to use an instance `backup`. Then, we finally developed the Ansible playbook and role to automate creating snapshot(s) of all instances within a specified tenant. I am very excited to move onto the next chapter where we will examine the process of migrating instances between Compute nodes. This is surely an administration task you will face while managing your OpenStack cloud. It is rather a controversial topic as well because many do not either know that this functionality exists within OpenStack or do not believe that this function works well. In the next chapter, we will try to clear up the unwarranted confusion by demonstrating how to manually migrate instance(s) and then take it a step further by automating it. For those of us who are cloud operators, the next chapter will be worth its value in gold. You do not want to skip the next chapter; it will certainly be worth it. `Chapter 6`, *Migrating Instances*, here we come!

6

Migrating Instances

In this chapter, we will cover the task of migrating instances using the native OpenStack capability built into the Compute service (Nova). As mentioned earlier the existence of this functionality is unknown by many. In this chapter, we will prove out this capability by demonstrating how to manually migrate instances. As well as, review the steps required to automate this task and finally create a playbook with roles to fully automate instance migration to a specified compute node.

This chapter will cover the following topics:

- Instance migration
- Automation considerations
- Coding the playbook and roles
- Playbook and role review

Instance migration

Whenever the topic of instance migration comes up, it normally ends in a spirited conversation among my OpenStack peers for various reasons. So as a responsible adult, I will go on recording and say that instance migration is not perfect.

It has its flaws and can be quirky at best. Migration, whether live or not, does have a practical use case to your OpenStack cloud. Within OpenStack, you have the capability of migrating instances from one compute node to another. Some of the reasons you may do this is for maintenance purposes and/or to rebalance resource utilization across the cloud. Also, keep in mind that there are multiple ways to clear out a compute node for maintenance and we will cover that in more detail in Chapter 8, *Setup Active-Active Regions*.

As mentioned earlier, the OpenStack Compute service (Nova) has the functionality to migrate instances in a traditional method and the ability to live-migrate an instance as well.

We will first examine the traditional migration method and its properties.

The traditional migration method will move an instance by shutting down that instance, coping the instance image/file to the next available compute node, starting the instance on the new node, and finally removing the instance from the original node. The areas to focus on in this method are:

- The instance is shut down
- The instance image/file will take time to copy to a new compute node
- New compute node's selection is done by Nova Scheduler; you cannot assign one without additional steps required
- The instance is then brought back online once the copying is complete

As you will note, this method can be considered by some as intrusive. The idea of shutting down an instance to move it is generally not a desirable scenario back in the virtualization days. Remember that we are in a new era, *the era of cloud and disposable resources.*

Since resources are readily available and you have the control to determine how to consume those resources, there should be no issues taking an instance offline. Right? Yes, I know that it will take a while to shake that *pet* mentality, you will get there. In the event the circumstances allow this, which normally means you did a good job distributing across your hypervisors the instances running your application(s), you can very easily use this method to migration instances.

A working example of the traditional instance migration command via the OpenStackClient CLI would be as follows:

```
$ openstack server migrate <instance>
$ openstack server migrate testinst
```

The other migration method would be to perform live instance migrations. This method would remove the requirement to shut down the instance as was highlighted in the traditional migration process described earlier. Instead of shutting down the instance, it is suspended (still in a running state) while the instance is reassigned to the new compute node. Much advancement has been made since the **Mitaka** release to improve this functionality. Such additions include the ability to track the migration progress, pause, or cancel a migration in flight and the possibility to exclude certain attached volumes.

There are additional system requirements needed in order to leverage the live migration functionality. Those requirements are as follows:

- Some sort of shared or external storage capability must exist between your compute nodes
- With live migration, you can select the new compute node, but you must assure that the new node has the resources required for the new instance
- The old and new compute nodes must have the same CPU; OpenStack releases before Kilo may encounter an issue if this is not the case

The first requirement is the most important one on the list, and it deserves some further explanation. The additional storage requirement can be covered in the following three different ways:

- The first way to satisfy the demand is to configure your hypervisors to store and have access to share storage for instance placement. This means that the instances are stored on the shared storage device and not on ephemeral storage. This could involve mounting NFS share on the compute node to be used to store instances or through fiber channel sharing LUN across the compute nodes, for example.
- The second approach to satisfying the shared/external storage requirement could be to leverage direct block storage where your instances are backed by image-based root disks.
- The third and final approach could be the boot from volume storage capability. This is where you are booting instances off of Cinder-based volumes. Of course, you would need the Block Storage service (Cinder) enabled and configured within your OpenStack cloud.

 A key message in relation to using the live migration capability within Nova is that your instances must exist on some sort of shared/external storage and cannot use ephemeral storage local to the compute node. More details on the required configuration can be found at `http://docs.o penstack.org/admin-guide/compute-configuring-migrations.html`.

A working example of an instance `server migrate` command via the Nova CLI would be as follows:

```
$ openstack server migrate --live=<new compute node> <instance>
$ openstack server migrate --live=compute01 testinst
```

As mentioned earlier, the whole concept of instance migration can range from being very simple all the way to being extremely complex. The hope here was you can now clearly understand what is required and the process followed during an instance migration. Let's now examine the process to manually migrating an instance using the CLI.

 For simplicity purposes, we will demonstrate the manual commands using the OpenStack CLI only.

Manually migrating instances

The Compute service (Nova) is responsible for managing the instance migration process. Nova behind the scenes will execute all the steps needed to reassign the instance(s) to the new node and the movement of the instance image/file. Just like with every OpenStack service, you must authenticate first either by sourcing the OpenRC file discussed in Chapter 1, *Introduction to OpenStack*, or by passing authentication parameters in-line with the command. The two tasks individually require different parameter values to be provided in order to successfully execute the command. The examples are mentioned here.

An instance migration using an OpenRC file:

```
$ source openrc
$ openstack server migrate <instance>
```

Instance migration passing authentication parameters in-line:

```
$ openstack --os-cloud=<cloud name> server migrate <instance>
```

After issuing the `openstack server migrate` command, I normally follow that up with the `openstack server show` command to report on the instance migration process. It is something that I normally would not use regularly when automating OpenStack tasks for obvious reasons. Since the migration process can take some time and we are executing the task manually, it helps to keep track of its progress.

Another way to check it on your migration would be to use the traditional Nova CLI with the `nova migration-list` command.

A real life working example with an OpenRC file could look something like this:

```
$ source openrc
$ openstack server list
$ openstack server migrate test-1ae02fae-93ca-4485-a797-e7f781a7a25b
$ nova migration-list
```

The output of the `nova migration-list` command would appear similar to this:

```
root@infra1_utility_container-c750da76:~# nova migration-list
+------------------+------------------+------------------+------------------+---------------+-----------+
| Source Node      | Dest Node        | Source Compute   | Dest Compute     | Dest Host     | Status    |
|                  |                  |                  |                  |               |           |
+------------------+------------------+------------------+------------------+---------------+-----------+
| 021579-compute03 | 021579-compute02 | 021579-compute03 | 021579-compute02 | 172.29.236.11 | confirmed |
T14:50:18.000000  |
| 021579-compute02 | 021579-compute03 | 021579-compute02 | 021579-compute03 | 172.29.236.12 | confirmed |
T13:42:07.000000  |
| 021579-compute02 | 021579-compute01 | 021579-compute02 | 021579-compute01 | 172.29.236.10 | finished  |
T13:44:57.000000  |
+------------------+------------------+------------------+------------------+---------------+-----------+
root@infra1_utility_container-c750da76:~#
```

The complete output provided in the earlier command will vary based on any previous migrations executed. The key information to focus on is the `Status` of the migration for the instance you just attempted to migrate. The status will be reported as either `migrating` or `finished`. Once the status is updated to `finished`, you can then confirm the migration of the instance.

After migration, the instance will be in a `VERIFY_RESIZE` state by default, whether or not you actually resized it.

```
root@infra1_utility_container-c750da76:~# nova show test-1ae02fae-93ca-4485-a797-e7f781a7a25b
+-------------------------------------+----------------------------------------------------------------+
| Property                            | Value                                                          |
+-------------------------------------+----------------------------------------------------------------+
| OS-DCF:diskConfig                   | AUTO                                                           |
| OS-EXT-AZ:availability_zone         | nova                                                          |
| OS-EXT-SRV-ATTR:host                | 021579-compute01                                              |
| OS-EXT-SRV-ATTR:hypervisor_hostname | 021579-compute01                                              |
| OS-EXT-SRV-ATTR:instance_name       | instance-00000002                                             |
| OS-EXT-STS:power_state              | 1                                                             |
| OS-EXT-STS:task_state               | -                                                             |
| OS-EXT-STS:vm_state                 | resized                                                       |
| OS-SRV-USG:launched_at              | 2015-09-17T13:45:00.000000                                    |
| OS-SRV-USG:terminated_at            | -                                                             |
| accessIPv4                          |                                                               |
| accessIPv6                          |                                                               |
| config_drive                        |                                                               |
| created                             | 2015-08-10T00:00:45Z                                          |
| flavor                              | m1.tiny (1)                                                   |
| hostId                              | d6d8be3a4f7132a048a15147fbe7275e7736b4124dcea0dc5032d989      |
| id                                  | 1ae02fae-93ca-4485-a797-e7f781a7a25b                          |
| image                               | cirros-0.3.3 (8681a786-ed10-403a-9f28-429d32f482ef)           |
| key_name                            | -                                                             |
| metadata                            | {}                                                            |
| name                                | test-1ae02fae-93ca-4485-a797-e7f781a7a25b                     |
| os-extended-volumes:volumes_attached| []                                                            |
| private-network network             | 10.1.100.3                                                    |
| progress                            | 0                                                             |
| security_groups                     | default                                                       |
| status                              | VERIFY_RESIZE                                                 |
| tenant_id                           | 903127b0aae141f298ffacf2cf8394dc                              |
| updated                             | 2015-09-17T13:44:57Z                                          |
| user_id                             | 8c1adba3f4cf49e3bdeb515492636e53                              |
+-------------------------------------+----------------------------------------------------------------+
root@infra1_utility_container-c750da76:~#
```

You would then need to execute the `openstack server resize` command to put the instance back to the `ACTIVE` state. The following example demonstrates this task:

```
$ openstack server resize
  --confirm test-1ae02fae-93ca-4485-a797-e7f781a7a25b
```

At this point, you are good to go! Your instance would have been migrated to a new compute node and now running in an `ACTIVE` state. For those of us who have learned to accept the traditional migration process, the next statement normally is, why can't I migrate an instance to a specific compute node using the nova migrate command? We will talk about this concern in the next section.

Migrating an instance to a specific compute node

The honest and straight answer to the earlier-mentioned question is that I have no clue why this capability was not included. Good thing is just like most things within OpenStack, there is always a way to get it to do what you want.

 Please be advised that the steps outlined next are 100% a workaround (mid-grade dirty workaround) and should not be used within a production environment without first executing multiple levels of testing to ensure expected functionality.

As covered in the sections earlier, you cannot migrate an instance to a specific compute node using the traditional migration method. This option just does not exist (hope that changes soon). However, you can trick the Nova Scheduler to place the instance on a selected compute node by disabling the other compute nodes. Nova Scheduler will then have no choice and migrate the instance to the compute node you selected. Yes, in your mind you just called me an idiot. Do not worry it is not as intrusive at it sounds on paper.

The OpenStack control plane services are designed to report on the status of the distributed components such as compute nodes and/or Cinder nodes. The report received is then stored within the OpenStack database, and this is how the control plane services know if a particular node is up or down. Similarly, the control plane services can also force a report of a nodes status.

The Compute service (Nova) is an example service that can force a report on the status of a compute node. This will simply mark a compute node as up or down within the database and never actually do anything physically to the compute node. All instances running on those compute nodes will remain running, and the overall functionality of the node will go unchanged. However, for the time the node is disabled within the database, it will prevent new instances to be created there. If you have a very busy continuously changing OpenStack cloud and are not using a segregated set of compute nodes, this workaround is probably not a wise idea.

Due to its intrusive nature, this felt like a perfect administrative task to try to automate. With something like this, timing and accuracy is very critical. Wasting something as small as a minute could equate to the failure of being able to create any number of new instances by your Cloud Consumers inside of your OpenStack cloud. For tasks of this nature, automation is a king. In the next few sections, we will review the required steps to automate this task.

Automation considerations

This task also did not require any new framework decisions. All the other automation decisions we reviewed previously carried over.

Before we start, it is worth noting that when automating a task such as this one (migrating an instance and disabling compute nodes) it is best to collect details concerning them both before and after the migration. Having those details will simplify the process of reversing your changes, if required. Yes, this will add additional tasks to your role making it slightly more complex but still well worth it.

With this said, we are now ready to proceed with creating our next playbook and role.

Coding the playbooks and roles

In this section, we will now create the playbook and role that will allow you to migrate an instance to a specific compute node using the traditional `openstack server migrate` command. Unlike the other tasks we have created thus far, there is really only one way to handle this task. We will take the steps outlined two sections earlier, automate them so that you only need to supply a few variable values, and then execute only one command.

This chapter started off talking about instance migration and how there are two options within Nova to handle this: traditional migration and live migration. The traditional migration process is really a one-step process, but in order to properly automate this task, we will need to add a few more steps to the process. The brief outline of the tasks we will have to create are:

1. List the compute nodes.
2. Collect premigration instance details.
3. Disable all compute nodes except for the one we want the instance to migrate to.
4. Migrate the instance.

5. Enable all compute nodes.

6. Confirm instance migration.

7. Collect postmigration instance details.

Role details

Since we are only creating a role in this example, we can start by the `main.yml` file within the role directory named `instance-migrate/tasks`. The beginning contents of this file will look like this:

```
---

- name: Retrieve hypervisor list
  shell: openstack --os-cloud="{{ CLOUD_NAME }}"
      hypervisor list | awk 'NR > 3' | awk '$4 != "{{ desthype }}"
      { print $4 }'
  register: hypelist
```

The first step of retrieving the complete list of compute nodes within your OpenStack cloud is pretty easy using the `openstack hypervisor list` command. Once you get those results, it is best to strip down the output to provide just the information you need. Again, we will do this using the `awk` command and pipe (|) symbol. You will notice that this is similar to how we did it in the previous chapter. Remember that the shell module is used here because we are executing commands that require shell-specific operations.

For this particular task, we have to get a bit magical with the `awk` commands:

```
awk 'NR > 3' | awk '$4 != "{{ desthype }}" { print $4 }'
```

Not only will it pull off the first three lines of the standard CLI output, it will also check the fourth column and print all the output except what matches what is passed in the `{{ desthype }}` variable. The consolidate output will then be registered into a variable named `hypelist`.

The next task will now collect premigration instance details that will be stored for later use within the role. The code to accomplish this looks as follows:

```
- name: Collect pre-migration instance details
  shell: openstack --os-cloud="{{ CLOUD_NAME }}"
      server list --name "{{ instance }}" --long | awk 'NR > 3' | awk '{
  print $16 }'
  register: preinststat
```

For this task, we are again using the OpenStackClient CLI to provide the instance details using the `openstack server list` command. You could as just as well use the `openstack server show` command to list the instance details. The distinct difference between the two commands is with the `openstack server list` command you can choose to display additional fields on the output. To do this, add the optional argument of `--long`.

In our particular case, we want to know the compute node that the particular instance is currently running on. Thus, we need to make sure that the `openstack server list` command looks like this:

```
openstack server list --name {{ instance }} --long
```

The third task will be to disable the compute node(s) that you do not want the instance to migrate to. Remember that we are only disabling the compute nodes within Nova and not physically changing the state of the compute node(s). The code to do this would look like this:

```
- name: Disable unselected hypervisors
  command: nova "{{ AUTH_S }}"
      service-disable "{{ item }}" nova-compute --reason '{{ migreason }}'
  with_items: "{{hypelist.stdout_lines}}"
```

With the use of the `nova service-disable` command, you can tell Nova to disable any particular Nova-related service on remote hosts. In order to have Nova Scheduler, ignore/skip a compute node you need to disable the nova-compute service. The command also requires a reason to be provided, of which will be stored in the Nova database for later reference if required. It is in this task where we will use the list of compute node(s) stored in the `hypelist` variable collected earlier.

Note that we will not disable the compute node that we want the instance to be migrated to as we have filtered it out of the list already.

Moving on to the fourth task, we will now execute the instance migration. At this point, only the compute node you have selected to receive the migrated instance is enabled and nothing special needs to be done in reference to the `openstack server migrate`. See the supporting code here:

```
- name: Migrate instance
  command: openstack --os-cloud="{{ CLOUD_NAME }}"
      server migrate "{{ instance }}"
```

Once the migration completes, we need to immediately enable back the compute node(s) that were disabled. One of the things I appreciate about OpenStack is if you are given a command to disable something, you are normally given a command to re-enable it. So we would simply execute the `nova service-enable` command. Again, we will use the `hypelist` variable to provide the list of compute node(s) to execute against. The code used is shown here:

```
- name: Enable the disabled hypervisors
  command: nova "{{ AUTH_S }}"
      service-enable "{{ item }}" nova-compute
  with_items: "{{hypelist.stdout_lines}}"
```

Now that the migration is complete and the compute node(s) are all enabled, we can focus on completing the instance migration process. The last step in an instance migration is to notify Nova that you acknowledge the instance was moved. At first glance, I could live without this step, but in hindsight, some sort of confirmation does make overall sense. Code for this task can be found here:

```
- name: Confirm instance migration
  command: openstack --os-cloud="{{ CLOUD_NAME }}"
      server resize --confirm "{{ instance }}"
```

The last two final tasks will be used to provide the individual running the playbook with a visual confirmation of what was done. Consider this more of an automation fail safe and less of a requirement. With such a complex administrative task as this it is always a good common practice to output some details of what was changed on your system:

```
- name: Collect post-migration instance details
  shell: openstack --os-cloud="{{ CLOUD_NAME }}"
      server list --name "{{ instance }}" --long | awk 'NR > 3' | awk '{
print $16 " and has a status of " $10 }' | awk 'NR == 1'
  register: postinststat
- name: Show instance location and status
  debug: msg="{{ instance }} was migrated from {{ item.0 }} to {{ item.1 }}"
  with_together:
    - "{{preinststat.stdout_lines}}"
    - "{{postinststat.stdout_lines}}"
```

These two tasks will first collect postmigration instance details and then use the information collected from the `preinststat` and `postinststat` variables to output to the screen a synopses of the changes done. The synapsis template used will be:

<instance migrated> was migrated from <compute node> to <compute node> and has a status of <instance current status>

Feel free to go in and change it to fit your needs. This is just my opinioned approach. It felt right to keep it simple while still supplying the pertinent details one would care about when handling a migration. Upon review of the playbook recap, if something went wrong and/or was implemented incorrectly you should be able to quickly target steps for remediation.

Variable details

Congratulations again, you have just completed your fourth OpenStack administration role. To support this role, we now need to create the variable file that will go along with it. The variable file named `main.yml`, which will be located in the `instance-migrate/vars` directory.

Keep in mind that the values defined in the variable file are intended to be changed before each execution for normal everyday use.

For this role, we kept it pretty simple on the variables front and only needed to define three variables:

```
---
desthype: 021579-compute02
instance: testG-2c00131c-c2c7-4eae-aa90-981e54ca7b04
migreason: "Migrating instance to new compute node"
```

Let's take a moment to break down each variable. The summary would be:

```
desthype   # this value would be the name of the compute node you wish
             to migrate the instance to

instance   # the name of the instance to be migrated

migreason: # a string encapsulated in quotes to explain the reason
             for migrating the instance (keep the string brief)
```

Playbook details

With the variable file completed, we can move on to creating the master playbook file. The file will be named `migrate.yml` and saved to the `root` directory of the `playbook` directory.

 The playbook and role names can be anything you choose. Specific names have been provided here in order to allow you to easily follow along and reference the completed code found in the GitHub repository. The only warning is whatever you decide to name the roles must remain uniform when referenced from within the playbook(s).

The contents of the `migrate.yml` file would be:

```
---
# This playbook used to migrate instance to specific compute node.

- hosts: util_container
  remote_user: root
  become: true
  roles:
    - instance-migrate
```

The summary of this file is as follows:

```
hosts        # the host or host group to execute the playbook against

remote_user  # the user to use when executing the playbook on the remote
 host(s)

become       # will tell Ansible to become the above user on the remote
 host(s)

roles        # provide a list of roles to execute as part of this playbook
```

Adding content to our host inventory file and the global variable file was already done two chapters ago, so we already have that part covered. The values defined earlier would remain the same. Here is a quick recap of how those files are configured.

The `hosts` file in the `root` directory of the playbook directory is:

```
[localhost]
localhost ansible_connection=local

[util_container]
172.29.236.199
```

The global variable file inside the `group_vars/` directory is:

```
# Here are variables related globally to the util_container host group

CLOUD_NAME: default

AUTH_S: --os-username {{ OS_USERNAME }} --os-password {{ OS_PASSWORD }} --
os-project-name {{ OS_TENANT_NAME }} --os-domain-name {{ OS_DOMAIN_NAME }}
--os-auth-url {{ OS_AUTH_URL }}

OS_USERNAME: admin
OS_PASSWORD: passwd
OS_TENANT_NAME: admin
OS_DOMAIN_NAME: default
OS_AUTH_URL: http://172.29.238.2:5000/v3
```

Word of caution

Due to the contents of this file it should be stored as a secure file within whatever code repository you may use to store your Ansible playbooks/roles. Gaining access to this information could compromise your OpenStack cloud security.

We are moving along very smoothly now, smile, you did it! Hopefully by this point everything is becoming a bit clearer. Keeping with our tradition, we will finish up the chapter with a quick review of the playbook and role just created.

Reviewing playbook and role

Let's jump right into examining the role we created, named `instance-migrate`. The completed role and file, named `main.yml`, located in the `instance-migrate/tasks` directory, looks like this:

```
---

- name: Retrieve hypervisor list
  shell: openstack --os-cloud="{{ CLOUD_NAME }}"
     hypervisor list | awk 'NR > 3' | awk '$4 != "{{ desthype }}" { print
$4 }'
  register: hypelist

- name: Collect pre-migration instance details
  shell: openstack --os-cloud="{{ CLOUD_NAME }}"
     server list --name "{{ instance }}" --long | awk 'NR > 3' | awk '{
print $16 }'
  register: preinststat
```

```
- name: Disable unselected hypervisors
  command: nova "{{ AUTH_S }}"
      service-disable "{{ item }}" nova-compute --reason '{{ migreason }}'
  with_items: "{{hypelist.stdout_lines}}"
- name: Migrate instance
  command: openstack --os-cloud="{{ CLOUD_NAME }}"
      server migrate "{{ instance }}"

- name: Enable the disabled hypervisors
  command: nova "{{ AUTH_S }}"
      service-enable "{{ item }}" nova-compute
  with_items: "{{hypelist.stdout_lines}}"

- name: Confirm instance migration
  command: openstack --os-cloud="{{ CLOUD_NAME }}"
      server resize --confirm "{{ instance }}"

- name: Collect post-migration instance details
  shell: openstack --os-cloud="{{ CLOUD_NAME }}"
      server list --name "{{ instance }}" --long | awk 'NR > 3' | awk '{
print $16 " and has a status of " $10 }' | awk 'NR == 1'
  register: postinststat
- name: Show instance location and status
  debug: msg="{{ instance }} was migrated from {{ item.0 }} to {{ item.1 }}"
  with_together:
    - "{{preinststat.stdout_lines}}"
    - "{{postinststat.stdout_lines}}"
```

The corresponding variable file, named main.yml, located in the instance-migrate/vars directory, for this role will look like this:

```
---
desthype: 021579-compute02
instance: testG-2c00131c-c2c7-4eae-aa90-981e54ca7b04
migreason: "Migrating instance to new compute node"
```

Next, the master playbook file, named migrate.yml, located in the root directory of the playbook directory, will look like this:

```
---
# This playbook used to migrate instance to specific compute node.

- hosts: util_container
  remote_user: root
  become: true
  roles:
    - instance-migrate
```

Following that we created the `hosts` file, which also is located in the `root` directory of the `playbook` directory:

```
[localhost]
localhost ansible_connection=local

[util_container]
172.29.236.199
```

Finally, creating the global variable file, named `util_container`, and saving it to the `group_vars/` directory of the playbook would complete the playbook:

```
# Here are variables related globally to the util_container host group

CLOUD_NAME: default

AUTH_S: --os-username {{ OS_USERNAME }} --os-password {{ OS_PASSWORD }} --
os-project-name {{ OS_TENANT_NAME }} --os-domain-name {{ OS_DOMAIN_NAME }}
--os-auth-url {{ OS_AUTH_URL }}

OS_USERNAME: admin
OS_PASSWORD: passwd
OS_TENANT_NAME: admin
OS_DOMAIN_NAME: default
OS_AUTH_URL: http://172.29.238.2:5000/v3
```

The complete set of code can again be found in the GitHub repository, https://github.com/os-admin-with-ansible/os-admin-with-ansible-v2.

We have finally landed on my most favorite part of creating Ansible playbooks and roles, which is to test out our great work. Fortunately for you, I have knocked out all the bugs already (wink wink). Assuming you have cloned the preceding GitHub repository, the command to test out the playbook from the Deployment node would be as follows:

```
$ cd os-admin-with-ansible-v2
$ ansible-playbook -i hosts migrate.yml
```

A sample of the playbook execution output can be viewed here:

```
root@021579-deploy01:~/ansiblefest-demo# ansible-playbook -i hosts migrate.yml

PLAY [util_container] ********************************************************

GATHERING FACTS *************************************************************
ok: [172.29.236.85]

TASK: [instance-migrate | Retrieve hypervisor list] *************************
changed: [172.29.236.85]

TASK: [instance-migrate | Collect pre-migration instance details] **********
changed: [172.29.236.85]

TASK: [instance-migrate | Disable unselected hypervisors] ******************
changed: [172.29.236.85] => (item=021579-compute01)
changed: [172.29.236.85] => (item=021579-compute03)

TASK: [instance-migrate | Migrate instance] *******************************
changed: [172.29.236.85]

TASK: [instance-migrate | Enable the disabled hypervisors] ****************
changed: [172.29.236.85] => (item=021579-compute01)
changed: [172.29.236.85] => (item=021579-compute03)

TASK: [instance-migrate | Confirm instance migration] ********************
changed: [172.29.236.85]

TASK: [instance-migrate | Collect post-migration instance details] *******
changed: [172.29.236.85]

TASK: [instance-migrate | Show instance location and status] *************
ok: [172.29.236.85] => (item=[u'021579-compute03', u'021579-compute02 and has a status of ACTIVE']) => {
    "item": [
        "021579-compute03",
        "021579-compute02 and has a status of ACTIVE"
    ],
    "msg": "test6-2c00131c-c2c7-4ege-aa90-981e54ca7b04 was migrated from 021579-compute03 to 021579-compute02 and has a status of ACTIVE"
}

PLAY RECAP *****************************************************************
172.29.236.85              : ok=9    changed=7    unreachable=0    failed=0
```

Summary

Nice to have completed yet another chapter covering real-life OpenStack administrative duties. The more you create playbooks and roles, the faster you will be able to create new code just by simply reusing the code created earlier for other purposes. Before this book is over, you will have a nice collection of playbooks/roles to reference for future Ansible automation.

Taking a moment to recap this chapter, you will recall that we covered what an instance migration is and why you would want to use this functionality. We reviewed the two possible migration methods traditional and live migration. You learned how to manually migrate an instance, as well as a workaround on how to use traditional migration to migrate an instance to a specific compute node. Finally, we created the Ansible playbook and role to automate that workaround approach. Overall instance maintenance and movement between compute nodes are continually improving. At some point you will not need to use some of the workaround mentioned in this chapter. Stay tuned for some great improvements!

The next chapter is a hot topic, as many of us have been exploring container technology. Particularly, we focused on how to consume and use containers while leveraging an OpenStack cloud. There are a few approaches now available, but the key is automating the process so that it is a reuseable function. In the next chapter, we will cover each approach and show the building blocks of how to accomplish this successfully. Grab another cup of coffee, do a quick stretch, and let's start Chapter 7, *Managing Containers on Your Cloud!*

7
Managing Containers on Your Cloud

In this chapter, we will cover one of the currently most discussed technology approaches, containers. The popularity around containers continues to build and rightfully so, who does not want an easier method of deploying applications and a consolidated approach to consuming computing resources? The best analogy I like to use, outside of the obvious shipping container on a ship analogy, when talking about containers is imagine putting all your code into a car or SUV. Then a vehicle carrier shows up at your door to pick up your vehicle. The maintenance for your vehicle will be minimal to none since the vehicle carrier is doing all the work. You only need to worry about making sure the vehicle carrier is working. This is the principle behind containers, we will go deeper into the container concept and also learn how you can leverage OpenStack and/or Ansible to build and deploy them. As in our usual fashion, as we go through each section we will be creating a few Ansible examples of how you can possibly manage various different container formats. We will cover the following topic in this chapter:

- Container concept explained
- Build and deploy containers
    - Building containers with Ansible Container
    - Deploying Kubernetes on OpenStack
    - Managing CoreOS and Docker with Ansible
    - Deploying Nova LXD on OpenStack
    - Reviewing playbooks and roles

The container concept explained

I have to believe that most folks that are into technology already know what containerization (aka containers) is, but in the freakish chance that my assumption is wrong, it felt like a good idea to start off by explaining what exactly it is. I will try to do my best not to just give you the Wikipedia definition and try to put some solid meaning around why the container model is a very useful addition to resource virtualization.

With the start of traditional virtualization, folks realized that I can sort of slice up my server into consumable chunks. No more is the need to dedicate a whole server to just being a web or application server. Quickly came on the adoption of cloud as many started to realize they were not using those virtualized resources correctly. Virtual machines sitting out there with no use or with too many resources that were not needed. One of the clouds major selling points is the fact that you can consume only what you need and that those resources are meant to be disposable, meaning use it and then dispose of it. All along while these technologies made consuming compute resources easier, none of them really helped in improving how you deploy applications.

Remember why you need those VM and instances, it is to run applications. What is the point of getting your hands on resources faster if it still takes days to still deploy a new application? In my opinion, this is the basis of why the containerization approach was crafted. Developers and system administrators (mainly system admins) wanted a more efficient method of deploying applications. I can personally remember the extremely painful process of deploying a new application or API. It consisted of attempting to step through a deployment document written by a developer, who most likely had never even logged into a server before or managed web/application server software before. Let's just say it was riddled with missed steps, wrong commands, and could never take into account any environment modifications that could be needed (such as dependent software versions).

Fast forwarding to the current time where you now have more options. There are quite a few different container technologies that now allow for developers to package up an application into a container and literally *ship it* to your container platform of choice. No more deployment documents, no more 2 AM deployment parties, and most importantly no more deployment mistakes. Since the container consists of a complete runtime environment for your applications all you need to manage is the container technology itself and the operating system it runs on. Containers are then also very easily moved between environments or across systems, as the only dependency is a server running the same container technology.

Now that you have some facts on containers you have to choose the platform that best suits your needs. Some of the most popular container technologies are Docker (`https://www.doc ker.com`), Kubernetes (`http://kubernetes.io`), CoreOS (`https://coreos.com`) and LXC/LXD (`https://linuxcontainers.org`).

So before you ask, you are probably thinking that since containers are relatively new can it be trusted, has the containerization concept been proven to work? Well the answer is yes, due to the simple fact that containers are not a new concept. Containers, or the concept of containerization, has been around for 10 years. The first container technology was LXC and it has been part of the Linux kernel for years now. With that said I would certainly say it has been tested true and certainly a technology to add to your organization's portfolio.

We can now embark on our journey of exploring containers further and strategize on how you can automate building and deploying them on your OpenStack cloud. The first path we need to go down in our journey is building our first container.

Building and deploying containers

In this section, we will learn how to design, build, and deploy containers to various container technologies. The breakdown of topics we will cover here are listed as follows:

- Building Containers with Ansible Container
- Deploying Kubernetes on OpenStack
- Managing CoreOS and Docker with Ansible
- Deploying Nova LXD on OpenStack

As mentioned previously, we will first start with learning how to build our first container using what I consider to be the easiest container tool there is, Ansible Container. Hope you are excited because I surely am, let's go!

Building containers with Ansible Container

What is Ansible Container?

> *Ansible describes Ansible Container as "the ultimate workflow for container development, testing, and deployment"*
>
> — (`https://docs.ansible.com/ansible-container`)

Consider it a workflow tool that enables you to not only build Docker images but also orchestrate the deployment of them and applications using Ansible playbooks. I will give you a second to pull yourself together now. Yes, our friends at Ansible have done it again and delivered another fantastic tool to put in our toolbox. No more having to be solely dependent on Dockerfile. All the power Ansible bring to the table can now be directly combined with building, running, deploying, and even pushing container images to the registry of choice. Everything you would like to know about Ansible Container can be found here: `http://docs.ansible.com/ansible-container`.

Just like with every other tool Ansible enables the center focus around Ansible Container, to be, simplicity and ease of use. Personally, I was able to install it and deploy my first container in just a few hours. One of the key features to Ansible Container is the ability to leverage shared container builds from Ansible Galaxy (`https://galaxy.ansible.com/int ro`) to get a jump start on designing your container images. Remember Open Source is all about sharing with the community.

Automation considerations

The first step is to get it installed, and since Ansible documentation is like none other there would be no need for me to reinvent the wheel. The installation options and details can be found at the following location: `http://docs.ansible.com/ansible-container/installa tion.html`. After you get it running the very next step I would suggest is to review the Getting Started guide found here: `http://docs.ansible.com/ansible-container/gettin g_started.html`.

We will now step through an example Ansible Container project that I have created to get started. This to me is the best way of learning a new technology. Spend some time with it, get your hands dirty, and come out more knowledgeable.

Step 1

Getting started with an Ansible Container project starts with something as simple as creating a new directory. Once the new directory has been created you then need to move into that directory and execute the Ansible Container initialization command. A working example of those commands is as follows:

```
$ mkdir elk-containers
$ cd elk-containers
$ ansible-container init
```

The output of the command would resemble this:

```
root@082108-deploy02:~# mkdir elk-containers
root@082108-deploy02:~# cd elk-containers/
root@082108-deploy02:~/elk-containers# ansible-container init
Ansible Container initialized.
root@082108-deploy02:~/elk-containers# ls
ansible
root@082108-deploy02:~/elk-containers# ls ansible
ansible.cfg  container.yml  main.yml  meta.yml  requirements.txt  requirements.yml
root@082108-deploy02:~/elk-containers#
```

In the example shown, our project will be named `elk-containers` and will be initialized in a directory named the same. Now that you have initialized your project, you will find that the Ansible Container files were created in a directory named `ansible`. The directory structure for your project will look like this:

```
ansible/
  container.yml
  main.yml
  meta.yml
  requirements.txt
  requirements.yml
  ansible.cfg
```

The files created here are skeleton files providing a shell to get you started. If you examine the two most important files, `container.yml` and `main.yml`, they will look something like this:

container.yml

```
version: "1"
services:
 # Add your containers here, specifying the base image you want to build
from
 # For example:
 #
 # web:
 #     image: ubuntu:trusty
   #  ports:
   #    - "80:80"
   #  command: ['/usr/bin/dumb-init', '/usr/sbin/apache2ctl', '-D',
'FOREGROUND']
   #    dev_overrides:
   #    environment:
```

```
#     - "DEBUG=1"
#
registries: {}
# Add optional registries used for deployment. For example:
# google:
#   url: https://gcr.io
#   namespace: my-cool-project-xxxxxx
```

main.yml

```
# This should be your Ansible playbooks to provision your containers.
# An inventory will be automatically created using the names of the
services
# from your container.yml file.
# Add any roles or other modules you'll need to this directory too.
# For many examples of roles, check out Ansible Galaxy:
https://galaxy.ansible.com/
#
---
- hosts: all
  gather_facts: false
```

Step 2

Now we are ready to either manually configure our container and/or leverage any of the many pre-packaged Ansible Container configs hosted on Ansible Galaxy. For our example here, we will pull down and use three different configs from Ansible Galaxy. Our example project will deploy three containers that collectively will be running the ELK stack (Elasticsearch, Logstash, and Kibana).

 Before executing the commands below, please make sure you have installed Ansible Container and all the prerequisite software. Refer to the Ansible Container installation instructions for details: `https://docs.ansi ble.com/ansible-container/installation.html`.

The commands to handle this are mentioned here; make sure you are in the `root` directory of your project directory when executed:

```
$ cd elk-containers
$ ansible-container install chouseknecht.kibana-container
$ ansible-container install chouseknecht.elasticsearch-container
$ ansible-container install chouseknecht.logstash-container
```

The output of the command would resemble this:

```
root@082108-deploy02:~/elk-containers# ansible-container install chouseknecht.elasticsearch-container
No DOCKER_HOST environment variable found. Assuming UNIX socket at /var/run/docker.sock
0.2: Pulling from ansible/ansible-container-builder
8d30e94188e7: Extracting [============================>                    ] 35.65 MB/70.59 MB
24cbd75f8b32: Download complete
d6ee161b4be5: Download complete
a4b49951d8df: Download complete
853ec44630ce: Download complete
b7e98f774514: Download complete
d787669f451c: Download complete
250fdf0b77c5: Download complete
33400106458e: Download complete
```

Once the base image is downloaded, Ansible Container will load it into a virtual container with all possible image dependencies to ready it to be built.

```
root@082108-deploy02:~/elk-containers# ansible-container install chouseknecht.kibana-container
No DOCKER_HOST environment variable found. Assuming UNIX socket at /var/run/docker.sock
Attaching to ansible_ansible-container_1
ansible-container_1  | - downloading role 'elasticsearch-container', owned by chouseknecht
ansible-container_1  | - downloading role from https://github.com/chouseknecht/elasticsearch-container/archive/master.tar.gz
ansible-container_1  | - extracting chouseknecht.elasticsearch-container to /etc/ansible/roles/chouseknecht.elasticsearch-container
ansible-container_1  | - chouseknecht.elasticsearch-container was installed successfully
ansible-container_1  | - dependency geerlingguy.java already pending installation.
ansible-container_1  | - downloading role 'java', owned by geerlingguy
ansible-container_1  | - downloading role from https://github.com/geerlingguy/ansible-role-java/archive/1.7.1.tar.gz
ansible-container_1  | - extracting geerlingguy.java to /etc/ansible/roles/geerlingguy.java
ansible-container_1  | - geerlingguy.java was installed successfully
ansible-container_1  | - downloading role 'logstash-container', owned by chouseknecht
ansible-container_1  | - downloading role from https://github.com/chouseknecht/logstash-container/archive/master.tar.gz
ansible-container_1  | - extracting chouseknecht.logstash-container to /etc/ansible/roles/chouseknecht.logstash-container
ansible-container_1  | - chouseknecht.logstash-container was installed successfully
ansible-container_1  | - dependency geerlingguy.java is already installed, skipping.
ansible-container_1  | - downloading role 'kibana-container', owned by chouseknecht
ansible-container_1  | - downloading role from https://github.com/chouseknecht/kibana-container/archive/master.tar.gz
ansible-container_1  | - extracting chouseknecht.kibana-container to /tmp/tmpKyRGaE/chouseknecht.kibana-container
ansible-container_1  | - chouseknecht.kibana-container was installed successfully
ansible_ansible-container_1 exited with code 0
root@082108-deploy02:~/elk-containers#
```

Step 3

Next we will now review what the previous `ansible-container` install commands did to our project. If we take a look at our `container.yml` and `main.yml` files now, we will notice that all the automation code we need to deploy the ELK stack to the containers is now there. Let's take a look at the changes to those files:

container.yml

```
version: '1'
services:
 kibana:
    image: centos:7
    ports:
    - 5601:5601
    user: kibana
    links:
    - elasticsearch
    working_dir: /opt/kibana/bin
    command: [./kibana]
 elasticsearch:
    image: centos:7
    ports:
    - 9200:9200
    expose:
    - 9300
    restart: always
    user: elasticsearch
    working_dir: /usr/share/elasticsearch/bin
    command: [./elasticsearch]
 logstash:
 image: centos:7
    ports:
    - 5044:5044
    links:
    - elasticsearch
    restart: always
    working_dir: /opt/logstash/bin
    command: [./logstash, agent, -f, /etc/logstash/conf.d]
    environment:
    - JAVACMD=/usr/bin/java

 # volumes:
   # - your_configuration_volume:/etc/logstash/conf.d
 # Add your containers here, specifying the base image you want to build
 from
 # For example:
 #
 # web:
 #    image: ubuntu:trusty
 #    ports:
 #       - "80:80"
   # command: ['/usr/bin/dumb-init', '/usr/sbin/apache2ctl', '-D',
 'FOREGROUND']
 #    dev_overrides:
```

```
#      environment:
#        - "DEBUG=1"
#
registries: {}
  # Add optional registries used for deployment. For example:
  # google:
#      url: https://gcr.io
  #      namespace: my-cool-project-xxxxxx
```

main.yml

```
- hosts: all
  gather_facts: false
- hosts: kibana
  roles:
  - role: chouseknecht.kibana-container
      kibana_host: 0.0.0.0
      kibana_port: 5601
      kibana_elasticsearch_url: http://elasticsearch:9200
      kibana_index: .kibana
      kibana_log_dest: stdout
      kibana_logging_silent: false
      kibana_logging_quiet: false
      kibana_logging_verbose: true
- hosts: elasticsearch
  roles:
  - role: chouseknecht.elasticsearch-container
      elasticsearch_network_host: 0.0.0.0
      elasticsearch_http_port: 9200
      elasticsearch_script_inline: true
      elasticsearch_script_indexed: true
      elasticsearch_data: /usr/share/elasticsearch/data
      elasticsearch_logs: /usr/share/elasticsearch/logs
      elasticsearch_config: /usr/share/elasticsearch/config
      java_home: ''
- hosts: logstash
  roles:
  - role: chouseknecht.logstash-container
      logstash_elasticsearch_hosts:
      - http://elasticsearch:9200

      logstash_listen_port_beats: 5044

      logstash_local_syslog_path: /var/log/syslog
      logstash_monitor_local_syslog: true

      logstash_ssl_dir: /etc/pki/logstash
    logstash_ssl_certificate_file: ''
```

```
logstash_ssl_key_file: ''

logstash_enabled_on_boot: yes

logstash_install_plugins:
- logstash-input-beats
```

The other file that we need to examine as well now is the `requirements.yml` file. Since we are using pre-packaged configs, a link to those configs will be added in this file:

requirements.yml

```
- src: chouseknecht.kibana-container
- src: chouseknecht.elasticsearch-container
- src: geerlingguy.java
- src: chouseknecht.logstash-container
```

At this point you have the option to make changes to the files if you have the need to adjust variables, specific application changes, or add additional orchestration steps. The best thing out of all of this is you can also choose not to make any changes at all. You can build and run this container project just as it is.

Step 4

In our final step, here we will take what we have designed, execute the Ansible Container build process, and finally deploy those containers locally. Again, for our example, we did not need to make any changes to container design files.

The build process is very powerful as all the container dependencies and orchestration will be implemented in order to create the container images. Those images will be used when you wish to deploy the containers. The following is the command to be used to build our containers:

```
$ ansible-container build
```

A snippet of the output of the command would resemble this:

```
root@82108-deploy02:~/elk-containers# ansible-container build
No DOCKER_HOST environment variable found. Assuming UNIX socket at /var/run/docker.sock
Starting Docker Compose engine to build your images...
Attaching to ansible_ansible-container_1
Cleaning up Ansible Container builder...
No image found for tag elk-containers-elasticsearch:latest, so building from scratch
No image found for tag elk-containers-logstash:latest, so building from scratch
No image found for tag elk-containers-kibana:latest, so building from scratch
7: Pulling from library/centos
88d40e6f1cff: Pull complete
Digest: sha256:b2f9d1c0ff5f87o4743104d099a3c561002ac500db1b9bfa82a783o46e0d366c
Status: Downloaded newer image for centos:7
Attaching to ansible_ansible-container_1, ansible_elasticsearch_1, ansible_logstash_1, ansible_kibana_1
ansible-container_1    | - downloading role 'elasticsearch-container', owned by chouseknecht
ansible-container_1    | - downloading role from https://github.com/chouseknecht/elasticsearch-container/archive/master.tar.gz
ansible-container_1    | - extracting chouseknecht.elasticsearch-container to /etc/ansible/roles/chouseknecht.elasticsearch-container
ansible-container_1    | - chouseknecht.elasticsearch-container was installed successfully
ansible-container_1    | - dependency geerlingguy.java already pending installation.
ansible-container_1    | - downloading role 'java', owned by geerlingguy
ansible-container_1    | - downloading role from https://github.com/geerlingguy/ansible-role-java/archive/1.7.1.tar.gz
ansible-container_1    | - extracting geerlingguy.java to /etc/ansible/roles/geerlingguy.java
ansible-container_1    | - geerlingguy.java was installed successfully
ansible-container_1    | - downloading role 'logstash-container', owned by chouseknecht
ansible-container_1    | - downloading role from https://github.com/chouseknecht/logstash-container/archive/master.tar.gz
ansible-container_1    | - extracting chouseknecht.logstash-container to /etc/ansible/roles/chouseknecht.logstash-container
ansible-container_1    | - chouseknecht.logstash-container was installed successfully
ansible-container_1    | - dependency geerlingguy.java is already installed, skipping.
ansible-container_1    | - downloading role 'kibana-container', owned by chouseknecht
ansible-container_1    | - downloading role from https://github.com/chouseknecht/kibana-container/archive/master.tar.gz
ansible-container_1    | - extracting chouseknecht.kibana-container to /etc/ansible/roles/chouseknecht.kibana-container
ansible-container_1    | - chouseknecht.kibana-container was installed successfully
ansible-container_1    | Host elasticsearch running
ansible-container_1    | Host logstash running
ansible-container_1    | Host kibana running
ansible-container_1    |
ansible-container_1    | PLAY [all] ************************************************************
ansible-container_1    |
ansible-container_1    | PLAY [elasticsearch] **************************************************
ansible-container_1    |
ansible-container_1    |
ansible-container_1    | TASK [chouseknecht.kibana-container : Create the kibana user] ********
ansible-container_1    | changed: [kibana]
ansible-container_1    |
ansible-container_1    | TASK [chouseknecht.kibana-container : Change kibana file ownership] **
ansible-container_1    | changed: [kibana]
ansible-container_1    |  [WARNING]: Consider using file module with owner rather than running chown
ansible-container_1    |
ansible-container_1    | TASK [chouseknecht.kibana-container : Set kibana file permissions] ***
ansible-container_1    | changed: [kibana]
ansible-container_1    |
ansible-container_1    | TASK [chouseknecht.kibana-container : Set log file permissions] ******
ansible-container_1    | changed: [kibana]
ansible-container_1    |
ansible-container_1    | TASK [chouseknecht.kibana-container : Template the config file] ******
ansible-container_1    | changed: [kibana]
ansible-container_1    |
ansible-container_1    | PLAY RECAP ***********************************************************
ansible-container_1    | elasticsearch              : ok=14   changed=8    unreachable=0    failed=0
ansible-container_1    | kibana                     : ok=9    changed=8    unreachable=0    failed=0
ansible-container_1    | logstash                   : ok=13   changed=8    unreachable=0    failed=0
ansible-container_1    |
ansible_ansible-container_1 exited with code 0
Aborting on container exit...
Stopping ansible_kibana_1 ... done
Stopping ansible_logstash_1 ... done
Stopping ansible_elasticsearch_1 ... done
Exporting built containers as images...
Committing image...
Exported elk-containers-elasticsearch with image ID sha256:ecf70318e3b6f3e7245398148e05ce4f298b38cabe9762d4893f1aeaec893562
Cleaning up elasticsearch build container...
Committing image...
Exported elk-containers-logstash with image ID sha256:001ba29dd7ff2302327c568fd54092ac31344dfc76c8oa63453e68d324b7e648
Cleaning up logstash build container...
Committing image...
Exported elk-containers-kibana with image ID sha256:547fdee02fd8f789fb0da935188b7f994b8e3d95f7ff18304ee42efd9d706064
Cleaning up kibana build container...
Cleaning up Ansible Container builder...
root@82108-deploy02:~/elk-containers#
```

Last, and certainly not least, we are ready to test out our brand new containers. As they say in the containerization world, *just ship it!*. Using Ansible Container to deploy the container images locally in order to test them out is yet another feature that just makes perfect sense. The `ansible-container run` command is what you will use to deploy the containers to your locally configured **Docker Engine** installation:

```
$ ansible-container run -d
```

Once run, the output of the command would resemble this, and we can confirm our container deployment by executing the `docker ps` command:

```
root@082108-deploy02:~/elk-containers# ansible-container run -d
No DOCKER_HOST environment variable found. Assuming UNIX socket at /var/run/docker.sock
Attaching to ansible_ansible-container_1
Cleaning up Ansible Container builder...
Deploying application in detached mode
root@082108-deploy02:~/elk-containers# docker ps
CONTAINER ID    IMAGE                              COMMAND                CREATED         STATUS
d01ed7202d80    elk-containers-logstash:latest     "./logstash agent -f " 2 minutes ago   Up About a minute
e792e09c461b    elk-containers-kibana:latest       "./kibana"             2 minutes ago   Up About a minute
24a6cd562f43    elk-containers-elasticsearch:latest "./elasticsearch"     2 minutes ago   Up About a minute
root@082108-deploy02:~/elk-containers#
```

As you can see, we have done well as we now have three containers running locally. *We did it!* Our very first container has been designed, configured, built, and deployed (all in less than an hour nevertheless). Before we move on we should probably stop or removed our containers for now. Please use the following command to either stop or remove your containers:

```
$ docker stop <container ID>
$ docker rm <container ID>
```

Deploying Kubernetes on OpenStack

At the time of writing, Kubernetes has been the market choice for container orchestration with being one of the top GitHub projects and emerging as the leading enterprise choice to manage containers. Some of the high-level features of Kubernetes are being able to perform rolling upgrades, zero downtime deployments, manage large-scale complex workloads, and highly available/fault tolerant out of the box. If you are looking to manage clusters of containers in a production environment, you should definitely give Kubernetes a go.

In that light, the question often arises, why would I want to run Kubernetes on a platform such as OpenStack? Many folks often forget that OpenStack is a hypervisor manager and not a hypervisor itself. OpenStack enables an operator to manage many different kinds of hypervisors, with container orchestration software being just another kind of hypervisor so to speak. Within OpenStack, you have a few ways you can choose to manage and deploy a Kubernetes cluster. It can be done via Magnum, the container management project within OpenStack. Another way is using Heat templates to manage the Kubernetes cluster as a stack. Lastly, you can use a GitHub project named **kargo**, which allows you to deploy Kubernetes using Ansible on many different systems and cloud platforms.

For our example here, we will cover the last option and use kargo to deploy Kubernetes on our OpenStack cloud. It did not feel like a good use of time to try and reinvent the wheel by creating our own Ansible playbooks/roles to deploy Kubernetes. The kargo project can be found at: `https://github.com/kubernetes-incubator/kargo`. There are instructions in the repository that will walk you through how to set up in order to run the setup playbook.

 Please keep in mind that kargo is an open source project, and just like every other open source project it is subject to change. Change could include reorganizing the repository layout, changes in deployment instructions and even depreciation. At the time of writing, the project is alive and working.

The OpenStack specific instructions can be found here: `https://github.com/kubernetes-incubator/kargo/blob/master/docs/openstack.md`. To get started, you would clone the kargo repository to your Utility container on your OpenStack cloud:

```
$ git clone https://github.com/kubernetes-incubator/kargo.git
$ cd kargo
```

Automation considerations

For the most part, the installation will go smoothly. I did have to tweak two small things to get the playbooks to finish successfully. The first tweak was within my OpenRC file. As you will note in the instructions, the second step is to source your OpenRC file before running the setup playbook. My file was missing two parameters that the playbook checked for; it was the `OS_TENANT_ID` and `OS_REGION_NAME` parameters. A working example of my OpenRC file is as follows:

```
# Ansible managed: /etc/ansible/roles/openstack_openrc/templates/openrc.j2
export LC_ALL=C

# COMMON CINDER ENVS
export CINDER_ENDPOINT_TYPE=publicURL
```

[113]

```
# COMMON NOVA ENVS
export NOVA_ENDPOINT_TYPE=publicURL

# COMMON OPENSTACK ENVS
export OS_ENDPOINT_TYPE=publicURL
export OS_USERNAME=admin
export OS_PASSWORD=passwd
export OS_PROJECT_NAME=admin
export OS_TENANT_NAME=admin
export OS_TENANT_ID=bcf04d870b4c469cb1728e71ef9a6422
export OS_AUTH_URL=https://192.168.0.249:5000/v3
export OS_NO_CACHE=1
export OS_USER_DOMAIN_NAME=Default
export OS_PROJECT_DOMAIN_NAME=Default
export OS_INTERFACE=publicURL
export OS_REGION_NAME=RegionOne

# For openstackclient
export OS_IDENTITY_API_VERSION=3
export OS_AUTH_VERSION=3
```

The other tweak that I had to make was adjusting how a particular Kubernetes dependent software container was pulled. The container repository tag was changed and the kargo project had not updated it yet. The update performed to the `roles/download/defaults/main.yml` file within the project. A snippet of the original file looked like this:

```
...
exechealthz_version: 1.1
exechealthz_image_repo: "gcr.io/google_containers/exechealthz-amd64"
exechealthz_image_tag: "{{ exechealthz_version }}"
hyperkube_image_repo: "quay.io/coreos/hyperkube"
hyperkube_image_tag: "{{ kube_version }}_coreos.0"
```

The file needed to be changed to look like this:

```
...
exechealthz_version: 1.1
exechealthz_image_repo: "gcr.io/google_containers/exechealthz-amd64"
exechealthz_image_tag: "{{ exechealthz_version }}"
hyperkube_image_repo: "quay.io/coreos/hyperkube"
hyperkube_image_tag: "v{{ kube_version }}_coreos.0"
```

With those two changes in place, all you need to do is spin up instances to serve as the Kubernetes master, etcd, and node. The instances can be any Linux-based operating system you wish. The way you layout your Kubernetes cluster varies on the type of environment and ultimately the use case. Reference architecture for a stable Kubernetes cluster would be to have two instances as masters, three instances as etcds, and leverage Ironic to deploy at least three bare metal servers to be the nodes. Of course, for testing purposes you can deploy the whole cluster as instances on your OpenStack cloud.

The next step would be to configure your inventory file to include the instances you spun up to act as your Kubernetes cluster. My inventory file was named `os-inventory`. A working example of an inventory file is as follows:

```
[kube-master]
kubes-1
kubes-2
[etcd]
kubes-3
kubes-4

[kube-node]
kubes-5
kubes-6
kubes-7

[k8s-cluster:children]
kube-node
kube-master
etcd
```

Believe it or not, you are now ready to run the setup playbook to deploy your Kubernetes cluster. The command to do so is as follows, please make sure you are within the `root` directory of the kargo repository:

```
$ ansible-playbook -i inventory/os-inventory -b cluster.yml
```

The installation will run for a bit, but at the end of it all you will have a working Kubernetes cluster to experiment with. We will now transition into another container orchestration technology and experiment with how we can use Ansible to manage containers while also leveraging OpenStack.

Managing CoreOS and Docker with Ansible

CoreOS seemed like another great fit to run on top of OpenStack because it is:

> *A lightweight Linux operating system designed for clustered deployments providing automation, security, and scalability for your most critical applications*
>
> — (https://coreos.com/why/#cluster)

CoreOS's focus is to provide an operating system that is by default cluster aware, making it a perfect fit for platforms such as container technologies. Docker was also an obvious choice for experimenting with containers since it was what made containers popular again. As well as, Docker has a vast variety of images ready to be pulled down and deployed as is. For our example, here we will review a very simple playbook that will deploy the ELK stack in containers on CoreOS.

Automation considerations

The first step in this process is to spin up a minimum of three instances with a flavor that has at least 2 GB of memory and a stable CoreOS image. Since I enjoy using Heat for things such as this, I spun up my instances using a Heat template. The template I created to accomplish this can be found here: https://github.com/wbentley15/openstack-heat-templates/tree/master/coreos. The command to then deploy the stack with Heat looked like this:

```
$ heat stack-create coreos --template-file=heat-coreos-prod.yaml --
  parameters="key-name=my-key;user-data=cloud-config-prod.yaml;
  network=24b9b982-b847-4d0e-9088-61acbf92a37f"
```

Coding the playbooks and roles

Once your CoreOS stack is online, you can execute the playbook we will now create. For this example, all the tasks will be in the playbook named `base.yml`, of which is located within the `root` directory of the `playbook` directory. The beginning contents of this file will look like this:

```
---
# This playbook deploys the ELK stack on CoreOS

- name: Bootstrap CoreOS
  hosts: coreos
  gather_facts: False
  roles:
  - defunctzombie.coreos-bootstrap
```

The very first task in the playbook is key to running packages such as Ansible against the target CoreOS instances. Since CoreOS is a minimal operating system it ships without any versions of Python. As we know, one of the major prerequisites to running Ansible against a host is to have Python installed. To circumvent this limitation we will use a role named `defunctzombie.coreos-bootstrap`, which will install `pypy` on our CoreOS instances. We will learn later how to tell Ansible where to find our Python interpreter on these nodes.

You can pull down this role from Galaxy by executing the following command:

```
$ ansible-galaxy install defunctzombie.coreos-bootstrap
```

The next two tasks will now set up the environment on the CoreOS instances to run Docker images as containers. Please make note that we will pin the `docker-py` and `docker-compose` packages to a particular version; this was due to a known bug with the `docker_image` and `docker_container` modules. This dependency can be removed once the bug is addressed, or those versions may need to be adjusted as time goes on:

```
- name: Deploy ELK Stack
  hosts: coreos
  remote_user: core
  become: false
  tasks:
    - name: Start etcd
      service: name=etcd.service state=started
      become: true

    - name: Install docker-py
      shell: /home/core/bin/pip install docker-py==1.9.0 docker-compose==1.8.0
```

The final remaining tasks will handle pulling down the Docker images for the ELK stack and then launching those containers on your CoreOS cluster:

```
- name: Pull Elasticsearch container
      docker_image: name=elasticsearch

    - name: Pull Kibana container
      docker_image: name=kibana
    - name: Pull Logstash container
     docker_image: name=logstash

  - name: Launch Elasticsearch container
    docker_container:
     name: elasticsearch-cont
        image: elasticsearch
        state: started

    - name: Launch Kibana container
       docker_container:
        name: kibana-cont
        image: kibana
        state: started
    - name: Launch Logstash container
      docker_container:
    name: logstash-cont
    image: logstash
    state: started
```

The Docker images are pulled down from repositories on `https://hub.docker.com` and then deployed on the CoreOS instances hosting Docker.

Our `hosts` file for this example was a bit unique again because of the custom Python interpreter we had to install for CoreOS. We were required to configure Ansible to use that alternative Python interpreter. In the following working example, you will find that we configured Ansible to use the Python interpreter located at `/home/core/bin/python` and the pip package at `/home/core/bin/pip`:

```
[coreos]
162.209.96.54

[coreos:vars]
ansible_ssh_user=core
ansible_python_interpreter=/home/core/bin/python
ansible_pip_interpreter=/home/core/bin/pip
```

Later in this chapter, we will wrap up by reviewing these playbooks and roles again, then also conclude with a test in order to see the finished results.

Deploying Nova LXD on OpenStack

Last, but certainly not least, we will conclude the chapter with the container option that really started it all, LXC, or rather its newer bigger brother, LXD. LXD is described as:

an container "hypervisor" and a new user experience for LXC

— (`https://www.ubuntu.com/cloud/lxd`)

The three major components of LXD are its system-wide daemon (**lxd**), command line client (**lxc**), and the OpenStack Nova plugin. It is that very plugin which will enable us to run LXD as a hypervisor under OpenStack control and use traditional OpenStack commands to spin up containers. With something like this you can literally run instances and containers on separate compute nodes under the same control plane. LXD is further described as being secure by design, scalable, intuitive, image, based, and the ability to perform live migrations.

Fortunately for us the Ansible gods have heard and answered our prayers. Within the **openstack-ansible project** (**OSA**) under the Newton release (and going forward) you can now deploy LXD as an alternative hypervisor to KVM. It is now as simple as editing two configuration files before deploying your OSA cloud. We will outline those changes and demonstrate how you can spin up your first LXD container using OpenStack.

Before we get started you should know that the detailed instructions for enabling LXD on OSA could be found here: `http://docs.openstack.org/developer/openstack-ansible-os_nova/`.

Automation considerations

An OSA deployment revolves around three main configuration files located within the `/etc/openstack_deploy` directory on your deployment node. You will need to edit the `user_variables.yml` and `user_secrets.yml` files. Starting with the `user_variables.yml` file, you will need to set the `nova_virt_type` variable to use LXD. A working example is as follows:

```
# This defaults to KVM, if you are deploying on a host that is not KVM
capable
# change this to your hypervisor type: IE "qemu", "lxc".
nova_virt_type: lxd
```

The second file that needs to be edited is the `user_secrets.yml` file. You will just need to supply a password for the LXD trust. An example of the line that needs to be edited is as follows:

```
# LXD Options for nova compute
lxd_trust_password:
```

In the event you are planning to set up a mixed compute node farm and wish to have both KVM and LXD hosts. You will need to edit the `openstack_user_config.yml` file and set the `nova_virt_type` for each host. A working example of how to configure this can be found in the preceding documentation link.

Now you can begin your OSA installation knowing that you will be able to spin up LXD containers as well as instances running on KVM. After the installation finishes you have one last step to complete. We now have to create an LXD compatible image that will be used when you spin up your containers. LXD requires the use of raw images, so we will pull down an image that meets those requirements. From within the Utility container on your OSA cloud, execute the following commands:

```
$ wget http://cloud-images.ubuntu.com/trusty/current/
  trusty-server-cloudimg-amd64-root.tar.gz
$ glance image-create --name=trusty-LXD --visibility=public --container-
  format=bare --disk-format=raw
  --file=trusty-server-cloudimg-amd64-root.tar.gz
```

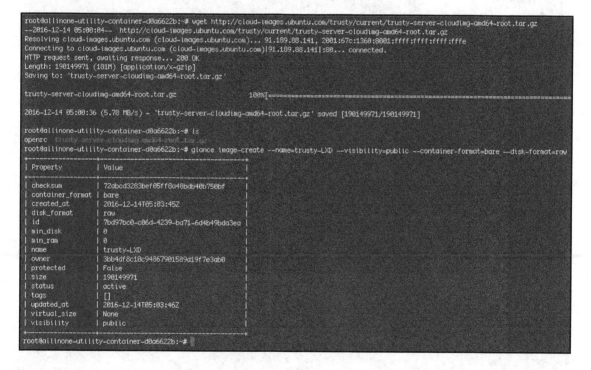

With your new image in place you are now ready to spin up your first LXD container. The LXD containers are managed in a similar manner as instances running on KVM. You can create a container via the Horizon dashboard or via the OpenStack Client CLI. For this example, we will use the OpenStack Client to create the containers. The following command will create your containers:

```
$ nova boot --image=<image name> --flavor=<flavor> --nic net-id=<network
ID> --security-group=<security group> --min-count <number of containers>
<container name>
```

```
$ nova boot --image=trusty-LXD --flavor=m1.small --nic net-
id=eb283939-2c65-4ecb-9d9f-cbbea9bf252c --security-group default --min-
count 3 first-lxd-container
```

You can count it as a success if your output looks similar to this:

```
+--------------------------------------+------------+--------+
| ID                                   | Name       | Status |
+--------------------------------------+------------+--------+
| 7bd97bc0-c06d-4239-ba71-6d4b49bda3ea | trusty-LXD | active |
+--------------------------------------+------------+--------+
root@allinone-utility-container-d0a6622b:~# nova boot --image=trusty-LXD --flavor=m1.small
+-------------------------------------+-------------------------+
| Property                            | Value                   |
+-------------------------------------+-------------------------+
| OS-DCF:diskConfig                   | MANUAL                  |
| OS-EXT-AZ:availability_zone         | nova                    |
| OS-EXT-SRV-ATTR:host                | -                       |
| OS-EXT-SRV-ATTR:hostname            | first-lxd-container-1   |
| OS-EXT-SRV-ATTR:hypervisor_hostname | -                       |
| OS-EXT-SRV-ATTR:instance_name       |                         |
| OS-EXT-SRV-ATTR:kernel_id           |                         |
| OS-EXT-SRV-ATTR:launch_index        | 0                       |
| OS-EXT-SRV-ATTR:ramdisk_id          |                         |
| OS-EXT-SRV-ATTR:reservation_id      | r-iogwhai0              |
| OS-EXT-SRV-ATTR:root_device_name    | -                       |
| OS-EXT-SRV-ATTR:user_data           | -                       |
| OS-EXT-STS:power_state              | 0                       |
| OS-EXT-STS:task_state               | scheduling              |
| OS-EXT-STS:vm_state                 | building                |
| OS-SRV-USG:launched_at              | -                       |
| OS-SRV-USG:terminated_at            | -                       |
```

You can then execute the `openstack server list` command to verify that your new containers are running.

```
root@allinone-utility-container-d0a6622b:~# openstack server list
WARNING: openstackclient.common.utils is deprecated and will be removed after Jun 2017. Please use osc_lib.utils.
+--------------------------------------+---------------------+--------+-----------------------------+------------+
| ID                                   | Name                | Status | Networks                    | Image Name |
+--------------------------------------+---------------------+--------+-----------------------------+------------+
| b72a81c2-5531-48b9-b2c7-aafcbfcec255 | first-lxd-container-3 | ACTIVE | private-network=10.1.100.8 | trusty-LXD |
| 63d2ef7d-f9f1-4bc0-801a-123a23aba29f | first-lxd-container-2 | ACTIVE | private-network=10.1.100.3 | trusty-LXD |
| 9cdaeb0d-c738-4112-8047-a1e1deef1471 | first-lxd-container-1 | ACTIVE | private-network=10.1.100.4 | trusty-LXD |
+--------------------------------------+---------------------+--------+-----------------------------+------------+
root@allinone-utility-container-d0a6622b:~#
```

Very cool my friend, you did great yet again! I know we covered a lot, but you are an old pro by now so no worries. Keeping with our tradition, we will finish up the chapter with a quick review of what we covered and what to expect in the next chapter.

Reviewing playbooks and roles

Let's jump right into examining the master playbook that we created earlier to deploy Docker containers on CoreOS called **ansible-coreos**. The completed playbook and file, named base.yml, located in the root of the ansible-coreos directory, looks like this:

```
---
# This playbook deploys the ELK stack on CoreOS

- name: Bootstrap CoreOS
  hosts: coreos
  gather_facts: False
  roles:
    - defunctzombie.coreos-bootstrap

- name: Deploy ELK Stack
  hosts: coreos
  remote_user: core
  become: false
  tasks:
    - name: Start etcd
      service: name=etcd.service state=started
      become: true

    - name: Install docker-py
      shell: /home/core/bin/pip install docker-py==1.9.0 docker-
compose==1.8.0

    - name: Pull Elasticsearch container
      docker_image: name=elasticsearch

    - name: Pull Kibana container
      docker_image: name=kibana
    - name: Pull Logstash container
      docker_image: name=logstash

    - name: Launch Elasticsearch container
      docker_container:
        name: elasticsearch-cont
        image: elasticsearch
        state: started
```

```
  - name: Launch Kibana container
   docker_container:
        name: kibana-cont
        image: kibana
        state: started
    - name: Launch Logstash container
       docker_container:
         name: logstash-cont
       image: logstash
    state: started
```

The corresponding role we pulled down from Galaxy is located in the `ansible-coreos/roles/defunctzombie.coreos-bootstrap/tasks` directory, and looks like this:

```
- name: Check if bootstrap is needed
 raw: stat $HOME/.bootstrapped
 register: need_bootstrap
 ignore_errors: True

- name: Run bootstrap.sh
 script: bootstrap.sh
 when: need_bootstrap | failed

- name: Check if we need to install pip
 shell: "{{ansible_python_interpreter}} -m pip --version"
 register: need_pip
 ignore_errors: True
 changed_when: false
 when: need_bootstrap | failed

- name: Copy get-pip.py
 copy: src=get-pip.py dest=~/get-pip.py
 when: need_pip | failed

- name: Install pip
 shell: "{{ansible_python_interpreter}} ~/get-pip.py"
 when: need_pip | failed

- name: Remove get-pip.py
 file: path=~/get-pip.py state=absent
 when: need_pip | failed

- name: Install pip launcher
 copy: src=runner dest=~/bin/pip mode=0755
 when: need_pip | failed
```

Finally, we created the `hosts` file, which also is located in the `root` directory of the `playbook` directory:

```
[coreos]
162.209.96.54

[coreos:vars]
ansible_ssh_user=core
ansible_python_interpreter=/home/core/bin/python
ansible_pip_interpreter=/home/core/bin/pip
```

 The complete set of code can again be found in the following GitHub repository: https://github.com/os-admin-with-ansible/os-admin-with-ansible-v2.

We are finally ready to give this playbook a try. Assuming you have cloned the previous GitHub repository, the command to test out the playbook from the deployment node would be as follows:

```
$ cd os-admin-with-ansible-v2
$ cd ansible-coreos
$ ansible-playbook -i hosts base.yml
```

Assuming all goes well, the output should resemble the snippet in the following screenshot:

```
TASK [defunctzombie.coreos-bootstrap : Remove get-pip.py] *********************
skipping: [162.209.96.54]

TASK [defunctzombie.coreos-bootstrap : Install pip launcher] ******************
skipping: [162.209.96.54]

PLAY [Deploy ELK Stack] *******************************************************

TASK [setup] ******************************************************************
ok: [162.209.96.54]

TASK [Start etcd] *************************************************************
changed: [162.209.96.54]

TASK [Install docker-py] ******************************************************
changed: [162.209.96.54]

TASK [Pull Elasticsearch container] *******************************************
changed: [162.209.96.54]

TASK [Pull Kibana container] **************************************************
changed: [162.209.96.54]

TASK [Pull Logstash container] ************************************************
changed: [162.209.96.54]

TASK [Launch Elasticsearch container] *****************************************
changed: [162.209.96.54]

TASK [Launch Kibana container] ************************************************
changed: [162.209.96.54]

TASK [Launch Logstash container] **********************************************
changed: [162.209.96.54]

PLAY RECAP ********************************************************************
162.209.96.54              : ok=10   changed=8   unreachable=0   failed=0

MMR1GWFD58:ansible-coreos wait7721$
```

Normally, I also like to take the extra step of verifying that the containers are running by executing the `docker ps` command on the CoreOS instances.

```
core@coreos-prod     docker start logstash-cont
logstash-cont
core@coreos-prod     docker start logstash-cont
logstash-cont
core@coreos-prod     docker start elasticsearch-cont
elasticsearch-cont
core@coreos-prod     docker ps -a
CONTAINER ID    IMAGE           COMMAND                CREATED         STATUS
c8109dcaedb3    logstash        "/docker-entrypoint.s" 12 minutes ago  Up 10 seconds
c7f02f6448a8    kibana          "/docker-entrypoint.s" 12 minutes ago  Up 12 minutes
4ba350dbaa0a    elasticsearch   "/docker-entrypoint.s" 12 minutes ago  Exited (1) 3 seconds ago
core@coreos-prod
```

Summary

Crossing the finish line does feel nice for sure. I hope that the raw power of what containers can offer you will inspire you to start deploying them on your OpenStack clouds. It always feels good to have options outside of the traditional VM's and instances.

Before concluding this chapter, let's take a moment to recap this chapter. We started the chapter with exploring the concept of Containerization and why it has become so very popular. You learned how to use Ansible Container to create our very first container image and build. We reviewed the kargo project that enables you to deploy Kubernetes using Ansible on multiple cloud platforms, including OpenStack. Next we demonstrated how to use Ansible to manage CoreOS running a Docker cluster on OpenStack. Lastly, we reviewed the configuration changes needed to deploy LXD with the **openstack-ansible** project.

The next chapter will also be a very interesting one because as a cloud operator you will eventually have to think about scaling up/out your cloud footprint. OpenStack has useful built-in features, which makes the process of scaling fairly easy and simple. In the next chapter, we will cover the concept of setting up active-active cloud regions and then take it up a notch with automating this task to alleviate the stress of scaling when the time arises. If you are ready for some unchartered waters, set a course for Chapter 8, *Setting Up Active-Active Regions*!

8

Setting Up Active-Active Regions

In this chapter, we will focus on demonstrating one of the very useful built-in features of OpenStack. This would be the capability of being able to centrally manage multiple OpenStack regions that could be running in separate geographical locations. The concept of regions within OpenStack is not a new one, but ask yourself whether you have ever actually seen it done. On many occasions, I found myself unclear on the steps needed to accomplish this. Well today is the day you will have a positive response to that question.

With stability and availability currently being popular topics within the OpenStack community, I thought it would be good to share a viable use case to accomplish cloud high availability. This will be just one of the many ways a cloud operator could set this up. As we may already know, OpenStack can meet numerous high-availability requirements. We will briefly review those scenarios and then transition to why you would use this functionality. As with all the previous chapters, we will then complete the chapter by demonstrating how to automate setting up Active-Active cloud regions using Ansible. We will cover the following topics in this chapter:

- Reviewing OpenStack high availability scenarios
- Why to use Active-Active cloud regions?
- Setting up Active-Active cloud regions
    - Creating and setting up Admin region
    - Configuring active regions' authentication
- Coding the playbooks and roles
- Reviewing the playbook and roles

Reviewing OpenStack high availability scenarios

This topic happens to be one of those I always enjoy discussing. **high availability** (**HA**) and disaster recovery always become very emotional conversations among IT folks for obvious reasons. Your neck is on the line, so to speak, to make sure that your organization's systems remain online in the event of a disaster/failure. In days of old local system, HA and cold (unused) disaster recovery sites were good enough. The current agility of cloud now offers up new and better options for system stability. Do not settle for the old solutions. You have options!

As repeated earlier, there are multiple ways to accomplish HA with OpenStack. We will outline three possible scenarios that I have found to be successful and would meet most organizations' HA requirements. The three possible scenarios are listed here with a diagram to add additional context:

- **Multiple data centers**: Multiple OpenStack regions are spanned across multiple geographically located data centers
- **Single data center**: Multiple OpenStack regions are within one data center
- **Availability zones**: Using paired availability zones within a single OpenStack region located within one data center

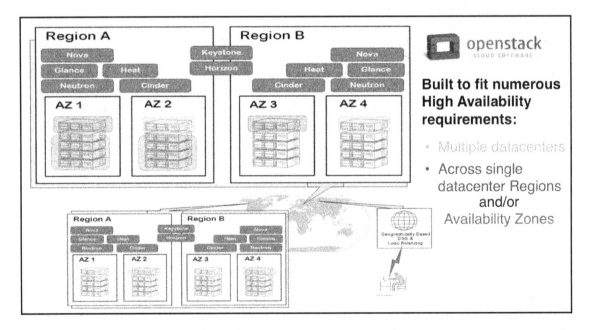

Multiple data centers

We would start with the most complex of the three scenarios. This scenario includes the concept of deploying multiple sets of OpenStack regions across numerous data centers and having them operate as one cloud system. While this may sound complicated, it is not as difficult as it sounds. The complexity comes into play when it comes time to tie them altogether and then of course when you go to support/manage them all. This model not only gives you HA across data centers (multiple Active-Active regions), but it also provides HA within each data center individually (independent Active-Active region). You would have to have multiple layers of failures in order to take your cloud offline.

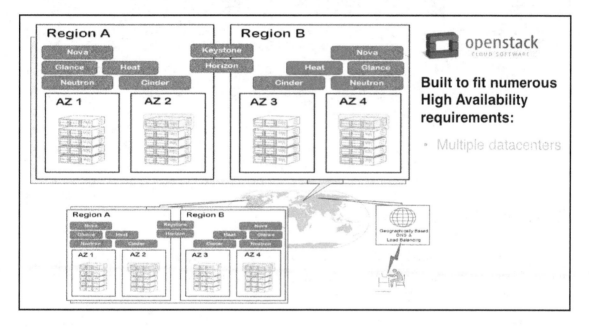

Single data center

Similar to the preceding scenario, with the major difference being that, it is only restricted to a single data center. In this scenario, you could deploy a single set of OpenStack Active-Active regions restrained to just one data center. This model would only provide HA within the data center where the regions are running. If that particular data center catches fire, your cloud would be **So Out of Luck (SOL)**.

If left with few options, this model could still save you from complete cloud failure.

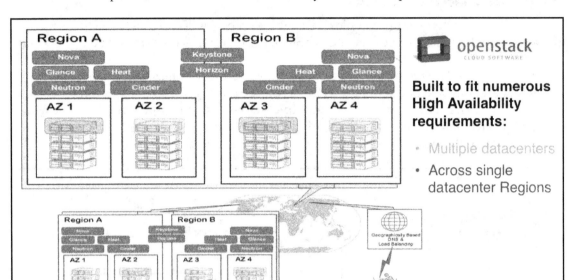

Availability Zones

This last scenario may be the simplest option but can certainly do the job in delivering guest-level HA. Yes, it does fall short if you are seeking to gain a true disaster recovery design. By leveraging multiple AZs, you can spread the instances across separate compute nodes using the anti-affinity filter, in essence providing the guest-level HA.

Now, let's focus on a simple paired down version of the multiple data center model we described earlier. We will review why you may be interested in using the Active-Active region approach.

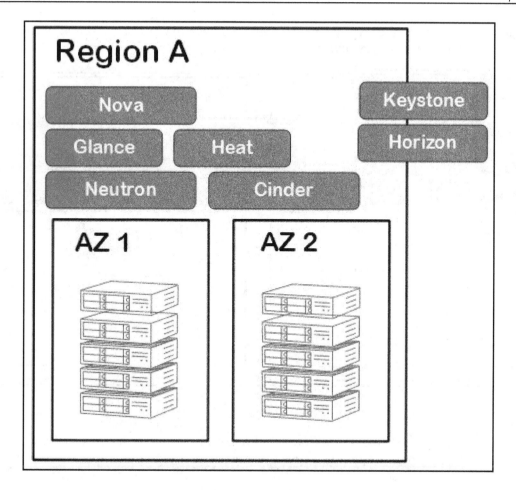

Why to use Active-Active cloud regions?

Outside of just the plain awesomeness of being able to actively use more than one OpenStack region, the Active-Active cloud region approach provides the best use of your overall cloud investment. No more are the days of having to perform DR tests simply because the second site is not regularly used. Plus you gain the added bonus of a centralized management region. A *win-win* situation all over the place.

So, let's go deeper into the architecture in order to deliver an OpenStack Active-Active region. The following diagram explains the architecture in its simplest form:

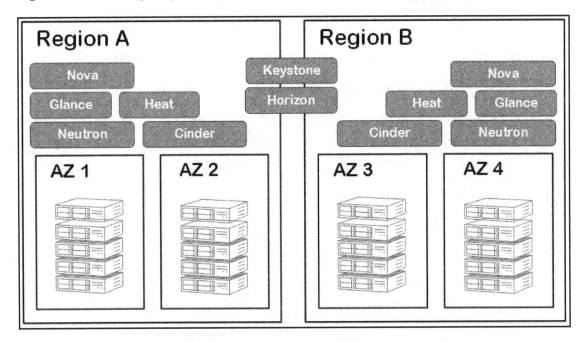

The components of the preceding architecture are:

- Two separate OpenStack cloud deployments, which in turn equates to two regions. In this example, we have **Region A** and **Region B**. These regions run the core OpenStack services except Keystone and Horizon. Each region can have any and as many complimentary AZs as you wish.
- Create another OpenStack region solely dedicated to hosting the Keystone and Horizon services. This region could be classified as the Admin region.
- Regions A and B would then leverage the Admin region to handle authentication and GUI web interface by centralizing user, tenant, and project management/creation as well as providing a single web dashboard to manage all the active regions.

Setting up Active-Active cloud regions

The process to implement it is relatively straightforward, but it does require distinct attention to detail. Outlining the steps beforehand I have found to be very useful and avoid missing steps. I have also learned that performing the changes manually (aka by hand) does not normally end well either. The process of editing the services configuration files does leave open the door of making edits by mistake, which leads to services that will not start. No good!!! Not even mentioning that it makes the process to implement take three times as long. First, we will review the steps manually and then in the following section, we will learn how to automate the setup process as much as possible. All I can say is thank heavens for Ansible!

In this section, we will review the manual steps to set up Active-Active OpenStack cloud regions. A brief snapshot of the steps is outlined here:

1. Inventory each region's endpoints and take note of the URLs.
2. Create service user accounts on the Admin region.
3. Create services on the Admin region.
4. Register each region's endpoints to the Admin region.
5. Adjust the Admin region's identity endpoint.
6. Configure each of the region's services to authenticate against the Admin region identity service instead of the local region's identity service.

Now, let's go step-by-step through each configuration step shown here demonstrating the working configuration examples.

Region endpoint inventory

This step would be a simple query of the endpoints of each region you want to include in the Active-Active setup. Since we are using **openstack-ansible** (**OSA**) to deploy our OpenStack clouds, you will need to connect into the utility container of each region in order to use the OpenStack CLI. Once connected and you source the OpenRC file, the command would be:

```
$ openstack endpoint list
```

The output of this command should look similar to this:

```
root@allinone-utility-container-249095b8:~# source openrc
root@allinone-utility-container-249095b8:~# openstack endpoint list
+----------------------------------+-----------+--------------+-----------------+---------+-----------+--------------------------------------------+
| ID                               | Region    | Service Name | Service Type    | Enabled | Interface | URL                                        |
+----------------------------------+-----------+--------------+-----------------+---------+-----------+--------------------------------------------+
| 0416e185b2444bbf9b591a374d3746b8 | RegionOne | keystone     | identity        | True    | internal  | http://172.30.238.2:5000/v3                |
| 139a189d843c44b8ac0b4f5cb6e17193 | RegionOne | heat-cfn     | cloudformation  | True    | internal  | http://172.30.238.2:8000/v1                |
| 225dda4edfcc4ca29e61d0af5cd078fc | RegionOne | neutron      | network         | True    | public    | http://172.30.238.2:9696                   |
| 2ce04bb5f4174b0283dba810c3496502 | RegionOne | nova         | compute         | True    | internal  | http://172.30.238.2:8774/v2.1/%(tenant_id)s |
| 3266246c60dfc49a4a443df8147fe5878| RegionOne | neutron      | network         | True    | admin     | http://172.30.238.2:9696                   |
| 348efac1bb194c97ae2e6730b8b2fd8d | RegionOne | heat         | orchestration   | True    | public    | http://172.30.238.2:8004/v1/%(tenant_id)s  |
| 363c61bb96b941a38fd486d7901963c4 | RegionOne | keystone     | identity        | True    | public    | http://172.30.238.2:5000/v3                |
| 3c05f1313e1b449c8a0c79b9bea3e4f5 | RegionOne | cinderv2     | volumev2        | True    | internal  | http://172.30.238.2:8776/v2/%(tenant_id)s  |
| 446615ae1a2464c77a27319a8735c33ae| RegionOne | keystone     | identity        | True    | admin     | http://172.30.238.2:35357/v3               |
| 636635c7eec64516879abf9f6bfd8d99 | RegionOne | cinderv2     | volumev2        | True    | public    | http://172.30.238.2:8776/v2/%(tenant_id)s  |
| 642eb7ed0f4240afa2de1ab475257046 | RegionOne | neutron      | network         | True    | internal  | http://172.30.238.2:9696                   |
| 6c13797e578c4bf29c4d146a937e88be | RegionOne | heat-cfn     | cloudformation  | True    | public    | http://172.30.238.2:8000/v1                |
| 6c544bb2e8cd416485bff724496db0c0 | RegionOne | nova         | compute         | True    | public    | http://172.30.238.2:8774/v2.1/%(tenant_id)s |
| 6e9701fb5db145d7878618fb0d30b0f2 | RegionOne | glance       | image           | True    | admin     | http://172.30.238.2:9292                   |
| 7720dd1889f84c3ab818067c22f30814 | RegionOne | nova         | compute         | True    | admin     | http://172.30.238.2:8774/v2.1/%(tenant_id)s |
| 94e7daddf29a34fe0a817a8fcc9cc5bb2| RegionOne | heat-cfn     | cloudformation  | True    | admin     | http://172.30.238.2:8000/v1                |
| 9879c69963e0438baab4b4ba6a9b8a18 | RegionOne | heat         | orchestration   | True    | internal  | http://172.30.238.2:8004/v1/%(tenant_id)s  |
| a3552efbbd544092b00d9b656c424100 | RegionOne | glance       | image           | True    | public    | http://172.30.238.2:9292                   |
| ae461419327c40ceab31240b3bf4d7fa | RegionOne | cinder       | volume          | True    | public    | http://172.30.238.2:8776/v1/%(tenant_id)s  |
| b39385349cb640029f38c4269cb1dc2e | RegionOne | cinder       | volume          | True    | admin     | http://172.30.238.2:8776/v1/%(tenant_id)s  |
| dff240d17bf14a2bb9b1af38da60d157 | RegionOne | glance       | image           | True    | internal  | http://172.30.238.2:9292                   |
| e270b472f18e4aeaaa397ad0d70ad268 | RegionOne | cinderv2     | volumev2        | True    | admin     | http://172.30.238.2:8776/v2/%(tenant_id)s  |
| ed85576c28354a6c9e064e081e2aa1d5 | RegionOne | heat         | orchestration   | True    | admin     | http://172.30.238.2:8004/v1/%(tenant_id)s  |
| fc17987f82304ca987bba2b9993f0ccc | RegionOne | cinder       | volume          | True    | internal  | http://172.30.238.2:8776/v1/%(tenant_id)s  |
+----------------------------------+-----------+--------------+-----------------+---------+-----------+--------------------------------------------+
root@allinone-utility-container-249095b8:~#
```

Keep in mind that our focus here is to just take note of the public endpoints available.

Since openstack-ansible installs the OpenStack services into LXC containers, you will need to know how to connect to each container for use of the CLI and to configure/maintain the services. The LXC command to list all the containers running on the control plane server is `lxc-ls -fancy`, and the output will look similar to the following:

```
root@010811-t01a:~# lxc-ls --fancy
NAME                                            STATE     IPV4                                         IPV6   AUTOSTART
allinone_cinder_api_container-7b00701a          RUNNING   10.0.3.58, 172.30.238.218, 172.30.246.180    -      YES (onboot, openstack)
allinone_cinder_scheduler_container-ee96fe66    RUNNING   10.0.3.173, 172.30.238.237                   -      YES (onboot, openstack)
allinone_galera_container-8f4c36a3              RUNNING   10.0.3.234, 172.30.238.52                    -      YES (onboot, openstack)
allinone_glance_container-2d39e7ca              RUNNING   10.0.3.65, 172.30.238.30, 172.30.246.184     -      YES (onboot, openstack)
allinone_heat_apis_container-a9f04733           RUNNING   10.0.3.119, 172.30.238.229                   -      YES (onboot, openstack)
allinone_heat_engine_container-3ceb134a         RUNNING   10.0.3.217, 172.30.238.153                   -      YES (onboot, openstack)
allinone_horizon_container-5183a2ca             RUNNING   10.0.3.51, 172.30.238.166                    -      YES (onboot, openstack)
allinone_keystone_container-4cc144f8            RUNNING   10.0.3.50, 172.30.238.248                    -      YES (onboot, openstack)
allinone_memcached_container-5fd0b502           RUNNING   10.0.3.174, 172.30.238.241                   -      YES (onboot, openstack)
allinone_neutron_agents_container-c71a1118      RUNNING   10.0.3.155, 172.30.238.41, 172.30.242.128    -      YES (onboot, openstack)
allinone_neutron_server_container-d088856c      RUNNING   10.0.3.39, 172.30.238.135                    -      YES (onboot, openstack)
allinone_nova_api_metadata_container-595ffe6c   RUNNING   10.0.3.141, 172.30.238.252                   -      YES (onboot, openstack)
allinone_nova_api_os_compute_container-f385cb47 RUNNING   10.0.3.139, 172.30.238.108                   -      YES (onboot, openstack)
allinone_nova_cert_container-0dfdf642           RUNNING   10.0.3.81, 172.30.238.219                    -      YES (onboot, openstack)
allinone_nova_conductor_container-c8f75b15      RUNNING   10.0.3.179, 172.30.238.234                   -      YES (onboot, openstack)
allinone_nova_console_container-0935000e        RUNNING   10.0.3.157, 172.30.238.205                   -      YES (onboot, openstack)
allinone_nova_scheduler_container-61cb68ed      RUNNING   10.0.3.131, 172.30.238.84                    -      YES (onboot, openstack)
allinone_rabbit_mq_container-bf8bf18c           RUNNING   10.0.3.192, 172.30.238.106                   -      YES (onboot, openstack)
allinone_repo_container-c410c787                RUNNING   10.0.3.167, 172.30.238.100                   -      YES (onboot, openstack)
allinone_rsyslog_container-891a674b             RUNNING   10.0.3.209, 172.30.238.160                   -      YES (onboot, openstack)
allinone_utility_container-249095b8             RUNNING   10.0.3.145, 172.30.238.214                   -      YES (onboot, openstack)
root@010811-t01a:~#
```

Admin region configurations

The next steps will now involve customizing the install and configuration of the Admin region. This will be your centralized management region servicing only authentication requests. The Admin region can exist in the same data center as one of the other regions or in an entirely separate region from the other. Obviously, network connectivity between the data centers would be required. Please follow the instructions given later in order to do this.

Creating service user accounts on the Admin region

At this point, you should have a functioning Admin region running only the identity service (Keystone) and the web dashboard (Horizon). Only those two services should be present and active. Since we want to use the Admin region to manage the other regions, you must make it aware of the other regions services and endpoints. This process starts with creating the service user accounts on the Admin region:

1. For this step, we will create the service user accounts using the CLI with the following command:

   ```
   $ openstack user create
     --project <project reserved for services>
     --password <user password> <user name>
   ```

   A working example of the command would look like this:

   ```
   $ openstack user create --project service
     --password passwd glance
   ```

2. Now we must assign the new user just created a role with the proper permissions. The CLI command to accomplish this is here:

   ```
   $ openstack role add --user <user name>
     --project <project reserved for services> <role>
   ```

   A working example of the command would look like this:

   ```
   openstack role add --user glance
   --project service admin
   ```

Now that we have the service user accounts created, we can transition on to the next step of registering the new services on the Admin region.

Creating services on the Admin region

In this step we are simply creating placeholders on the Admin region for the services running on the active regions. Remember that the active regions have the other core services running on them and the Admin region will handle the authentication for them. The Admin region then has to be aware of the services.

The services will be registered on the Admin region using the following command:

```
$ openstack service create --name <service name>
  --description "<service description>" <service type>
```

A working example of the command would look like this:

```
openstack service create --name glance
--description "Glance Image Service" image
```

The next step will now be to register the active regions endpoints on the Admin region. This step requires a level of precision, as the endpoint URL is what the Admin region will use to make functional calls. If the URL is incorrect or mistyped, the service will be considered down per the Admin region.

Registering each region's endpoints to the Admin region

The process of registering the active region's endpoints involves using the endpoint inventory we started with earlier. The key points here are that you must use the IP address from the public endpoints of each region. The IP address assigned to the public endpoint needs to be a public IP address (accessible over the Internet) or an internal IP address accessible between each data center. Again, the Admin region will use this URL to make service calls, so the endpoint must be reachable.

You will be required to register two types of endpoints: **public** and **internal**. I discovered this key component during the setup process. Some of the OpenStack services leverage the internal endpoints solely, whereas others will use the public endpoints. In order to avoid any issues, we will register both. Technically, there is zero risk to registering both and it is a good practice.

An example of the command to register the service is as follows:

```
$ openstack endpoint create --region <region name>
  <service name> <service type> <endpoint url>
```

A set of working examples of the command would look like this:

```
$ openstack endpoint create --region alpha glance
  internal
  http://127.0.0.1:9292
$ openstack endpoint create --region alpha glance
  public
  http://127.0.0.1:9292
```

The preceding step needs to be repeated for every active region you wish to join under the Admin region. As depicted in the earlier example, we would execute this step for **Region A** and **Region B**.

Adjusting the Admin regions' identity endpoint

The last step in setting up the Admin region is to make sure that the active regions can successfully connect to the identity service running there. The same principle shared earlier about having to expose the services public endpoint applies here as well for Keystone . Every cloud setup may differ slightly, so this step may not be required for all clouds.

In order to evaluate if you need to make this adjustment, execute the following command and determine if the public and admin endpoints have local IP addresses configured for the URL:

```
$ openstack endpoint list --service identity
```

If the output looks similar to this, you must disable the public and admin endpoints after creating new ones with either a public IP or IP address accessible between data centers. More details on how to handle this will be shared here:

```
root@010811-t01a:~# lxc-ls --fancy
NAME                                           STATE    IPV4                                        IPV6  AUTOSTART
allinone_cinder_api_container-7b00701a         RUNNING  10.0.3.58, 172.30.238.218, 172.30.246.180   -     YES (onboot, openstack)
allinone_cinder_scheduler_container-ee96fe66   RUNNING  10.0.3.173, 172.30.238.237                  -     YES (onboot, openstack)
allinone_galera_container-8f4c36a3             RUNNING  10.0.3.234, 172.30.238.52                   -     YES (onboot, openstack)
allinone_glance_container-2d39e7ca             RUNNING  10.0.3.65, 172.30.238.38, 172.30.246.184    -     YES (onboot, openstack)
allinone_heat_apis_container-a9f04733          RUNNING  10.0.3.119, 172.30.238.229                  -     YES (onboot, openstack)
allinone_heat_engine_container-3ceb134a        RUNNING  10.0.3.217, 172.30.238.153                  -     YES (onboot, openstack)
allinone_horizon_container-5183a2ca            RUNNING  10.0.3.51, 172.30.238.166                   -     YES (onboot, openstack)
allinone_keystone_container-4cc144f8           RUNNING  10.0.3.50, 172.30.238.248                   -     YES (onboot, openstack)
allinone_memcached_container-5fd0b502          RUNNING  10.0.3.174, 172.30.238.241                  -     YES (onboot, openstack)
allinone_neutron_agents_container-c71a1118     RUNNING  10.0.3.155, 172.30.238.41, 172.30.242.128   -     YES (onboot, openstack)
allinone_neutron_server_container-d088856c     RUNNING  10.0.3.39, 172.30.238.135                   -     YES (onboot, openstack)
allinone_nova_api_metadata_container-595ffe6c  RUNNING  10.0.3.141, 172.30.238.252                  -     YES (onboot, openstack)
allinone_nova_api_os_compute_container-f385cb47 RUNNING 10.0.3.139, 172.30.238.108                  -     YES (onboot, openstack)
allinone_nova_cert_container-0dfdf642          RUNNING  10.0.3.81, 172.30.238.219                   -     YES (onboot, openstack)
allinone_nova_conductor_container-c8f75b15     RUNNING  10.0.3.179, 172.30.238.234                  -     YES (onboot, openstack)
allinone_nova_console_container-0935000e       RUNNING  10.0.3.157, 172.30.238.205                  -     YES (onboot, openstack)
allinone_nova_scheduler_container-61cb68ed     RUNNING  10.0.3.131, 172.30.238.84                   -     YES (onboot, openstack)
allinone_rabbit_mq_container-bf8bf18c          RUNNING  10.0.3.192, 172.30.238.106                  -     YES (onboot, openstack)
allinone_repo_container-c410c787               RUNNING  10.0.3.167, 172.30.238.100                  -     YES (onboot, openstack)
allinone_rsyslog_container-891a674b            RUNNING  10.0.3.209, 172.30.238.160                  -     YES (onboot, openstack)
allinone_utility_container-249095b8            RUNNING  10.0.3.145, 172.30.238.214                  -     YES (onboot, openstack)
root@010811-t01a:~# ssh 172.30.238.214
Welcome to Ubuntu 14.04.5 LTS (GNU/Linux 3.13.0-91-generic x86_64)

 * Documentation:  https://help.ubuntu.com/
Last login: Sun Nov  6 15:02:07 2016 from 172.30.238.2
root@allinone-utility-container-249095b8:~# source openrc
root@allinone-utility-container-249095b8:~# openstack endpoint list --service identity
+----------------------------------+-----------+--------------+--------------+---------+-----------+------------------------------+
| ID                               | Region    | Service Name | Service Type | Enabled | Interface | URL                          |
+----------------------------------+-----------+--------------+--------------+---------+-----------+------------------------------+
| 0416e185b2444bbf9b591a374d3746b8 | RegionOne | keystone     | identity     | True    | internal  | http://172.30.238.2:5000/v3  |
| 363c61bb96b941a38fd486d7901963c4 | RegionOne | keystone     | identity     | True    | public    | http://172.30.238.2:5000/v3  |
| 44615ae1a2464c77a27319a8735c33ae | RegionOne | keystone     | identity     | True    | admin     | http://172.30.238.2:35357/v3 |
+----------------------------------+-----------+--------------+--------------+---------+-----------+------------------------------+
root@allinone-utility-container-249095b8:~#
```

In order to create the new public and admin endpoints and then disable the current ones, you would execute the following commands:

```
# Add public Keystone endpoint
$ openstack endpoint create --region <region name>
  keystone public <endpoint url>
# Add an additional admin Keystone endpoint
$ openstack endpoint create --region <region name>
  keystone admin <endpoint url>
# Disable the original public Keystone endpoint
  with the local IP address
  configured (URL will have a non-routable address)
$ openstack endpoint set --disable <endpoint-id>
# Disable the original admin Keystone endpoint with
```

```
    the local IP address configured
    (URL will have a non-routable address)
$ openstack endpoint set --disable <endpoint-id>
```

Once completed, upon issuing the `openstack endpoint list --service identity` command, the output should look similar to this:

```
allinone_cinder_api_container-4d0aab39          RUNNING 10.0.3.104, 172.32.238.130, 172.32.246.97    -   YES (onboot, openstack)
allinone_cinder_scheduler_container-aaba387e    RUNNING 10.0.3.26, 172.32.238.74                     -   YES (onboot, openstack)
allinone_galera_container-ac213797              RUNNING 10.0.3.209, 172.32.238.120                    -   YES (onboot, openstack)
allinone_glance_container-6f441d81              RUNNING 10.0.3.186, 172.32.238.168, 172.32.246.228   -   YES (onboot, openstack)
allinone_heat_apis_container-c02a9488           RUNNING 10.0.3.198, 172.32.238.110                   -   YES (onboot, openstack)
allinone_heat_engine_container-04b5dc50         RUNNING 10.0.3.71, 172.32.238.166                    -   YES (onboot, openstack)
allinone_horizon_container-8ed929e6             RUNNING 10.0.3.101, 172.32.238.81                    -   YES (onboot, openstack)
allinone_keystone_container-48c12645            RUNNING 10.0.3.126, 172.32.238.124                   -   YES (onboot, openstack)
allinone_memcached_container-009a7dd6           RUNNING 10.0.3.112, 172.32.238.60                    -   YES (onboot, openstack)
allinone_neutron_agents_container-9552b4f5      RUNNING 10.0.3.131, 172.32.238.90, 172.32.242.177    -   YES (onboot, openstack)
allinone_neutron_server_container-813818f6      RUNNING 10.0.3.84, 172.32.238.142                    -   YES (onboot, openstack)
allinone_nova_api_metadata_container-c1d8fd0b   RUNNING 10.0.3.147, 172.32.238.190                   -   YES (onboot, openstack)
allinone_nova_api_os_compute_container-e329b517 RUNNING 10.0.3.114, 172.32.238.28                    -   YES (onboot, openstack)
allinone_nova_cert_container-6b59a075           RUNNING 10.0.3.229, 172.32.238.205                   -   YES (onboot, openstack)
allinone_nova_conductor_container-52c2e75b      RUNNING 10.0.3.49, 172.32.238.246                    -   YES (onboot, openstack)
allinone_nova_console_container-b7a21d4c        RUNNING 10.0.3.110, 172.32.238.187                   -   YES (onboot, openstack)
allinone_nova_scheduler_container-090939af      RUNNING 10.0.3.237, 172.32.238.213                   -   YES (onboot, openstack)
allinone_rabbit_mq_container-3d6f6afa           RUNNING 10.0.3.141, 172.32.238.85                    -   YES (onboot, openstack)
allinone_repo_container-f7f140bc                RUNNING 10.0.3.64, 172.32.238.201                    -   YES (onboot, openstack)
allinone_rsyslog_container-2860f687             RUNNING 10.0.3.40, 172.32.238.174                    -   YES (onboot, openstack)
allinone_utility_container-2ccdcbf6             RUNNING 10.0.3.130, 172.32.238.133                   -   YES (onboot, openstack)
root@010811-t01admin:~# ssh 172.32.238.133
Welcome to Ubuntu 14.04.5 LTS (GNU/Linux 3.13.0-91-generic x86_64)

 * Documentation:  https://help.ubuntu.com/
Last login: Thu Oct 27 08:02:42 2016 from 172.32.238.2
root@allinone-utility-container-2ccdcbf6:~# source openrc
root@allinone-utility-container-2ccdcbf6:~# openstack endpoint list --service identity
+----------------------------------+-----------+--------------+--------------+---------+-----------+-------------------------------+
| ID                               | Region    | Service Name | Service Type | Enabled | Interface | URL                           |
+----------------------------------+-----------+--------------+--------------+---------+-----------+-------------------------------+
| 0874f553186d4156bc0cf54818880fb5 | RegionOne | keystone     | identity     | True    | internal  | http://172.32.238.2:5000/v3   |
| b2345c924dc24f139e6c39af6695663e | RegionOne | keystone     | identity     | True    | admin     | http://166.78.18.131:35357/v3 |
| c2a75ca9547e4eaf947fed7bc8238c19 | RegionOne | keystone     | identity     | True    | public    | http://166.78.18.131:5000/v3  |
| c3a2bf5d76cc4cc1bb12c15c149dc7c3 | RegionOne | keystone     | identity     | False   | admin     | http://172.32.238.2:35357/v3  |
| f0a372e5a6434fcc8965df1f1ae1dc8d | RegionOne | keystone     | identity     | False   | public    | http://172.32.238.2:5000/v3   |
+----------------------------------+-----------+--------------+--------------+---------+-----------+-------------------------------+
root@allinone-utility-container-2ccdcbf6:~#
```

Active region configurations

This section will include the steps to setting up the active regions that will be part of your Active-Active cloud design. These are the regions running the core OpenStack services. At this point, we have the Admin region set up to communicate with these active regions. Now we must configure the core services to authenticate through the Admin region instead of using the local identity service (Keystone).

You cannot deploy an OpenStack cloud without first setting up a local identity service. The identity service has to be the first service installed and thus would exist on the active regions. To have the services not use the local identity service, you must reconfigure each service. Simply disabling the local identity service is not enough to make this work. The process of reconfiguring each core service includes editing the configuration file. As already mentioned earlier, editing the service configuration files leaves the door open to make edits by mistake that could then lead to that service not starting.

This is where you must work smarter and not harder. Ask yourself: Is there a tool that can assist in such a task? Yes, the answer yet again is Ansible! Ansible can assist in making those many service configuration changes greatly minimizing typos. In Chapter 2, *Introduction to Ansible,* we briefly discussed Ansible ad hoc commands. Ad hoc commands allow direct module commands to be run without wrapping the task into a playbook or role.

A basic example of an ad hoc command would look like this:

```
$ ansible <host> -m <module> -a <module arguments>
```

In our situation, we need to connect to a specific container running on the control plane and make a change to that services configuration file. This needs to be repeated for each core service running on that active region. Good news is that we can leverage the dynamic inventory part of the openstack-ansible deployment to make the overall process simpler. Let's use the following example as a sample to show how it can be accomplished.

In this example, we will attempt to make the required changes to the image service (Glance) on the Alpha region. So, the things we know are:

- You must connect to the Glance container
- Using the `sed` command, we will need to leverage the shell Ansible module
- We have a `sed` command prepared that will change the `auth_url` value within the `glance-api.conf` file

A further breakdown of the command parameters would now be:

```
host = glance_container
module = shell
adhoc command = sed -i 's+^auth_url = <current IP>:35357+auth_url =
http://<alpha region IP>:35357+' /etc/glance/glance-api.conf
```

 In order to leverage the dynamic inventory feature part of the *openstack-ansible install,* you must execute these commands from the deployment node (the node used to deploy the region). As well as, you much execute the commands while within the /opt/openstack-ansible/playbooks directory.

A working example of the command would then look like this:

```
$ ansible glance_container -m shell -a "sed -i
's+^auth_url = http://172.30.238.2:35357+auth_url =
 http://166.78.18.131:35357+' /etc/glance/glance-api.conf"
```

You can use the preceding principles to make the required changes to all the services on your active regions. Make sure to remember to restart the services after the configuration file changes are made.

```
$ ansible nova_scheduler_container -m service -a
   "name=nova-scheduler state=restarted"
```

Coding the playbooks and roles

In this section, we will now create the playbooks and roles to set up the Admin region. We will also then outline the Ansible ad hoc commands needed to complete the other steps to set up the Active-Active clouds. When creating Ansible automation code for something of this nature, I typically like to create multiple tasks broken out into separate roles. This format allows you to be able to reuse roles created with other playbooks. We will end up with two playbooks and two roles to automate the steps to set up the Admin region. In the end, we will then recap the playbooks consuming those roles.

In the other half of this section, we will also outline the Ansible ad hoc commands needed to complete the other steps to set up the Active-Active clouds. You could surely collect the commands together to create playbooks and roles. I felt that this would be a few hundred lines of unnecessary code, so I went with drafting the commands and using search-and-replace.

Setting up the Admin region

The first role we will create will include those tasks needed to configure the Admin region. The name of the file will be `main.yml`, located within the role directory named `config-admin-region/tasks`. The contents of this file will look like this:

```
---

- name: Create users
  os_user:
    cloud: "{{CLOUD_NAME}}"
    state: present
    name: "{{ item.0 }}"
    password: "{{ item.1 }}"
    default_project: "{{ servicesproject }}"
    domain: default
  with_together:
    - "{{userid}}"
    - "{{passwdss}}"

- name: Assign user to specified role in designated environment
  os_user_role:
    cloud: "{{CLOUD_NAME}}"
    user: "{{ item.0 }}"
    role: "{{ urole }}"
    project: "{{ servicesproject }}"
  with_together:
    - "{{userid}}"
- name: Register the new services on the Admin region
  shell: openstack --os-cloud="{{ CLOUD_NAME }}"
      service create --name "{{ item.0 }}" --description "{{ item.1 }}" "{{
servicetype }}"
  with_together:
    - "{{userid}}"
    - "{{descrip}}"
```

The first task will create the service user accounts on the Admin region. The second task will then assign the admin role to the users just created. The last task will then create the placeholder for the services hosted on the active regions.

The next role to be created will handle the tasks of registering each region's endpoints within the Admin region. Just as with the previous role, the file will be named `main.yml`, located within the role directory named `register-endpoints/tasks`. The contents of this file will look like this:

```
---
```

```
- name: Register the region service endpoints on the Admin region
  shell: openstack --os-cloud="{{ CLOUD_NAME }}"
      service endpoint create --region "{{ item.1 }}" "{{ item.0 }}" "{{
item.2 }}" "{{ item.3 }}"
  with_together:
    - "{{endpointname}}"
    - "{{regionname}}"
    - "{{endpointtype}}"
    - "{{endpointurl}}"
```

The role only has one task that is to use the CLI command of service endpoint create to register the endpoints. In this circumstance, we used the with_together parameter so that we could loop through the four parameters defined as variables. This way you can rerun the playbook with only having to adjust the variable values. As in our case, we would need to run this playbook twice, one for internal endpoints and one for the public endpoints.

To support these roles, we now need to create the variable file that will go along with it. For these two roles, we will use role-defined variable files to simplify things a bit. The variable file will be stored within the role directory inside another directory named vars. The file inside of that directory will be named main.yml.

The contents of the variable file corresponding to the role named config-admin-region will look like this:

```
---
userid: [ 'glance', 'nova', 'neutron', 'heat' ]
passwdss: [ 'passwd', 'passwd', 'passwd', 'passwd' ]
descrip: [ 'Glance Image Service', 'Nova Compute Service', 'Neutron Network
Service', 'Heat Orchestration Service' ]
servicetype: [ 'image', 'compute', 'network', 'orchestration' ]

servicesproject: service
urole: admin
```

The contents of the second variable file corresponding to the role named register-endpoints will look like this:

```
---
endpointname: [ 'glance', 'nova', 'neutron', 'heat' ]
regionname: alpha
endpointtype: internal
endpointurl: [ 'http://<alpha region IP>:9292', 'http://<alpha region
IP>:8774/v2.1/%\(tenant_id\)s', 'http://<alpha region IP>:9696',
'http://<alpha region IP>:8004/v1/%\(tenant_id\)s' ]
```

Keep in mind that the values defined in the variable file are intended to be changed before each execution for normal everyday use.

Let's take a moment to break down the variables and their expected use. The summary would be:

```
userid          # name of the user to create

passwdss        # passwords for the users being created

descript        # description for the service being registered

servicetype     # type of service being registered

servicesproject # name of the project where the services user accounts are
associated

urole           # name of the role to associate with the user

endpointname    # service name of the endpoint being registered
regionname      # name of the region

endpointtype    # the type of endpoint being registered

endpointurl     # the url of the endpoint
```

With the variable file completed, we can move on to creating the master playbook files. For our demonstration, I decided to break up the playbook files into two separate files. This was totally my choice and could be combined into one file with no issues. I felt that having two separate master playbooks would make it easier to rerun when you need to register multiple sets of endpoints. The list of playbook files will be described here:

```
config-admin.yml
   config-admin-region

register-endpoints.yml
   register-endpoints
```

The playbook and role names can be anything you choose. Specific names have been provided here in order to allow you to easily follow along and reference the completed code found in the GitHub repository. The only warning is whatever you decide to name the roles must remain uniform when referenced from within the playbook(s).

Setting up Active regions

This is where we will use the Ansible ad hoc commands to finish up the configuration. As mentioned earlier, we will leverage the dynamic inventory capabilities part of openstack-ansible deployment model to accomplish this. These commands will reconfigure the OpenStack services to use the Admin region to authenticate. Here is a snippet of the commands that you need to execute to reconfigure the core services on each region becoming part of the Active-Active region setup. The full list of commands can be found in the **os-admin-with-ansible/os-admin-with-ansible-v2** Github repository within a file named `configure-region-authentication.txt` located on the `root` directory.

```
## Glance
ansible glance_container -m shell -a "sed -i 's+^auth_url =
http://172.30.238.2:35357+auth_url = http://<admin region IP>:35357+'
/etc/glance/glance-api.conf"
ansible glance_container -m shell -a "sed -i 's+^auth_url =
http://172.30.238.2:35357+auth_url = http://<admin region IP>:35357+'
/etc/glance/glance-registry.conf"
ansible glance_container -m shell -a "sed -i 's+^auth_url =
http://172.30.238.2:5000/v3+auth_url = http://<admin region IP>:5000/v3+'
/etc/glance/glance-cache.conf"

ansible glance_container -m shell -a "sed -i 's+^auth_uri =
http://172.30.238.2:5000+auth_uri = http://<admin region IP>:5000+'
/etc/glance/glance-api.conf"
ansible glance_container -m shell -a "sed -i 's+^auth_uri =
http://172.30.238.2:5000+auth_uri = http://<admin region IP>:5000+'
/etc/glance/glance-registry.conf"

ansible glance_container -m shell -a "service glance-api restart"
ansible glance_container -m shell -a "service glance-registry restart"
```

The approach I have found to be the best and most efficient is to do a search for the placeholder of `<admin region IP>` and replace it with the public IP or internal IP associated with Admin region. You can do it with any text editor and it can be set with commands to execute against any region.

Well done everyone! You just configured your OpenStack cloud with multiple regions that are all active. As always, for us to keep up with our tradition, we will finish up the chapter with a quick review of the playbook and role just created.

Reviewing playbooks and roles

Let's jump right into examining the roles we created.

The completed role and file, named `main.yml`, located in the `config-admin-region/tasks` directory, looks like this:

```
---

- name: Create users
 os_user:
  cloud: "{{CLOUD_NAME}}"
  state: present
  name: "{{ item.0 }}"
  password: "{{ item.1 }}"
  default_project: "{{ servicesproject }}"
  domain: default
 with_together:
  - "{{userid}}"
  - "{{passwdss}}"

- name: Assign user to specified role in designated environment
 os_user_role:
  cloud: "{{CLOUD_NAME}}"
  user: "{{ item.0 }}"
  role: "{{ urole }}"
  project: "{{ servicesproject }}"
 with_together:
  - "{{userid}}"
- name: Register the new services on the Admin region
 shell: openstack --os-cloud="{{ CLOUD_NAME }}"
     service create --name "{{ item.0 }}" --description "{{ item.1 }}" "{{
servicetype }}"
 with_together:
  - "{{userid}}"
  - "{{descrip}}"
```

The completed role and file, named `main.yml`, located in the `register-endpoints/tasks` directory, looks like this:

```
---

- name: Register the region service endpoints on the Admin region
 shell: openstack --os-cloud="{{ CLOUD_NAME }}"
     service endpoint create --region "{{ item.1 }}" "{{ item.0 }}" "{{
item.2 }}" "{{ item.3 }}"
 with_together:
```

```
- "{{endpointname}}"
- "{{regionname}}"
- "{{endpointtype}}"
- "{{endpointurl}}"
```

The corresponding role local variable files are both named `main.yml` and are saved to the `vars` directory of the role:

```
# variables for config-admin-region

---
userid: [ 'glance', 'nova', 'neutron', 'heat' ]
passwdss: [ 'passwd', 'passwd', 'passwd', 'passwd' ]
descrip: [ 'Glance Image Service', 'Nova Compute Service', 'Neutron Network
Service', 'Heat Orchestration Service' ]
servicetype: [ 'image', 'compute', 'network', 'orchestration' ]

servicesproject: service
urole: admin



# variables for register-endpoints

---
endpointname: [ 'glance', 'nova', 'neutron', 'heat' ]
regionname: alpha
endpointtype: internal
endpointurl: [ 'http://<alpha region IP>:9292', 'http://<alpha region
IP>:8774/v2.1/%\(tenant_id\)s', 'http://<alpha region IP>:9696',
'http://<alpha region IP>:8004/v1/%\(tenant_id\)s' ]
```

Next, we created the following master playbook files; all will be located in the `root` directory of the `playbook` directory:

- `config-admin.yml`:

  ```
  ---
  # This playbook used to demo OpenStack Juno user, role and project
  features.

  - hosts: util_container
  remote_user: root
  become: true
  roles:
      - config-admin-region
  ```

- `register-endpoints.yml`:

```
---
# This playbook used to demo OpenStack Juno user, role and project
features.

- hosts: util_container
  remote_user: root
  become: true
  roles:
    - register-endpoints
```

In the end of this, we created the `hosts` file, which also is located in the `root` directory of the `playbook` directory:

```
[localhost]
localhost ansible_connection=local

[util_container]
172.29.236.224
```

The complete set of code can again be found in the GitHub repository at https://github.com/os-admin-with-ansible/os-admin-with-ansible-v2.

Now the fun part, time to test out our new playbooks and roles. You will need to also execute the additional ad hoc commands described earlier to completely test out this functionality. Assuming that you have cloned the GitHub repository mentioned earlier, the command to test out the playbook from the Deployment node would be as follows:

```
$ ansible-playbook -i hosts config-admin.yml
$ ansible-playbook -i hosts register-endpoints.yml
```

Next, you would execute the commands found in the file named `configure-region-authentication.txt`, located in the `root` directory of the `playbook` directory. If all went well you would be able to log into the web dashboard of the Admin region and see the following when you click on the project name on the top header of the page:

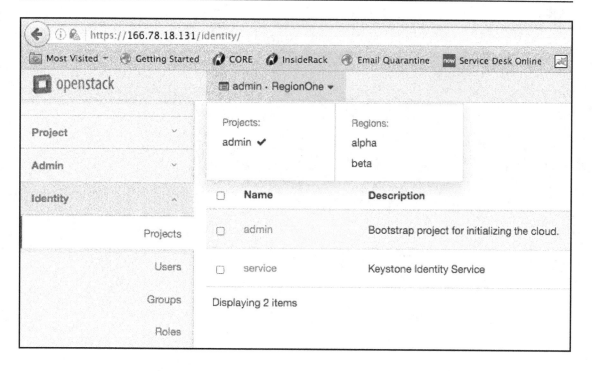

Summary

Yes! You just set up your OpenStack cloud in an Active-Active design. The flexibility and reliability you just gained solves for most mainstream HA requirements. Have fun jumping between the regions and separating out your application resources within one or two clicks. Before concluding this chapter, let's take a moment to recap this chapter. We talked through the benefits that OpenStack offers out of the box to handle high-availability requirements. Then, we transitioned to some possible reasons you would want to use Active-Active cloud regions. Next, we walked through the steps of how to set up the Active-Active cloud regions. Finally, we developed Ansible playbooks and roles to automate setting up the Admin region.

The next chapter happens to also be something that came in as a customer demand for a pretty large OpenStack cloud. There is no cloud operator out there who does not want to know or have a complete inventory of their cloud. Tracking resources, auditing users, and recapping network utilization are just a few things part of the daily/weekly routine for us. Imagine that you can have a complete report created in one command. Is it possible? Well I am not telling. You will have to read on to Chapter 9, *Inventory your Cloud*, to find out.

9

Inventory Your Cloud

I am very excited to dive into this chapter, as we will focus on a topic that is considered challenging when administering an OpenStack cloud. Gathering metrics around the system being consumed is a pretty high item on the daily priority list. The bad news is OpenStack does not necessarily make this an easy task. In OpenStack's defense, I will say that there has been great work done around the most recent releases to improve this. The new **OpenStackClient** (**OSC**) has done a better job, allowing the Cloud Operator to pull together various different metrics about the cloud.

In the meantime, there are ways to collect these metrics in an ad hoc fashion and then put a very simple report together. As with most things related to OpenStack, there are a few ways to approach it. After attempting to do this using multiple methods, I found that it was easily accomplished by executing queries against the OpenStack databases. I know, I know…no one wants to touch the database. In my past life, I used to be a DBA, and one thing I learned from that experience is that simple clearly defined queries are harmless to any database. Combining that theory and using a tool such as Ansible to pull all the information collected together is a winning combo. In this chapter, we will review how you can dynamically inventory various pieces of your OpenStack cloud resources. We will learn what metrics are of value and how that information can be stored for later reference as well. This is an extremely powerful tool to have as a Cloud operator.

- Collecting cloud metrics
    - User report
    - Project report
    - Network report
    - Volume report
    - Cloud-at-a-Glance report
    - Coding the playbook and roles
- Review playbook and role

Collecting cloud metrics

The first step in this process is to determine what metrics are important to you. Keep in mind that the approach outlined here is just my very opinioned way of tackling this. As a Cloud operator, you may have a different way you wish to handle this. Use this as a springboard to get you started.

From my experience, it is best to pull together user, project, network, and volume metrics. Then, take all that data, combine it together, and output total cloud utilization metrics. This is very similar to what the Horizon dashboard does. While it is easy to log into Horizon and do a quick review, what if you wanted to provide a comprehensive report to your leadership? Or maybe you wanted to take a point-in-time snapshot to compare cloud utilization over a time period. There may be a possible requirement to audit your cloud one day. There exists no real easy way to do this in a report format without using a third-party tool. All these scenarios can be satisfied using the approach outlined next.

Let's start at the beginning by taking a look at collecting user metrics first.

User report

Capturing information about the users defined in your cloud is probably the simplest metric to record. When the day comes that you have to audit your cloud for compliance and security reasons, you will note that you list out the users and even list out the roles assigned to users, but not both together. Similarly, you can list out the users in a project but not the role assigned to that user for that project together. You can see where I am going with this. It would only make sense to have a complete list of the users with their IDs, what roles they are assigned, and to what project(s) they have access to in one report. Using the following simple database query you can very easily attain this information:

```
USE keystone;
SELECT local_user.user_id, local_user.name as username, role.name as role,
project.name as tenant from local_user
INNER JOIN assignment ON
local_user.user_id=assignment.actor_id INNER JOIN
role ON assignment.role_id=role.id INNER JOIN
project ON assignment.target_id=project.id
ORDER BY tenant;
```

This query will combine data from four different tables within the database named **keystone**. The keystone database is the owner of all the user-related data. Each table within the database has at least one primary key that can be used to link the data together. Here is a quick breakdown of the tables used here and their functions:

```
User        # contains the raw user information such as ID, name,
              password and etc.
Assignment  # contains the role assignment for all users
Role        # is the list of roles created/available
Project     # contains the list of projects/tenants created/available
```

In this example, we will focus on only pulling back the necessary columns from the four tables. To make things a bit easier to read, we also renamed a few of the column labels. Finally, we will sort the data by the project name in an ascending order to give us a clean and easy output. I promise not to go much further into the weeds on this SQL query. This is a book on OpenStack and Ansible, not SQL commands, right?

 Always try to use the ID column of the table to link data from other tables when possible. The ID column will always be a unique value that will provide reliable data correlation every time. Using columns that contain item name values could eventually cause a conflict if a row exists in the table with duplicate values. Even OpenStack on the whole uses this approach, as you will note that anything created within OpenStack has an ID associated with it.

After executing this query, the output will look something similar to this:

```
+----------------------------------+----------------------+------------------+---------+
| user_id                          | username             | role             | tenant  |
+----------------------------------+----------------------+------------------+---------+
| 08a7cb13da35409bbd4ea7a38305a79f | admin                | heat_stack_owner | admin   |
| 08a7cb13da35409bbd4ea7a38305a79f | admin                | admin            | admin   |
| d16645f79cac4d65a04b92c9751d3a81 | stack_domain_admin   | admin            | heat    |
| e2c6e044d622473984e1ca7cfb604a2a | trustee_domain_admin | admin            | magnum  |
| 71b3d6a1c5b84bdb9271a74653a34047 | keystone             | admin            | service |
| 4c36b1dd8b7649d1a24521ed637d2e3b | cinder               | admin            | service |
| c2a86e0cc8bb400f95fd633bf025aa57 | neutron              | admin            | service |
| ed200031a8314b91b46815153db98725 | heat                 | admin            | service |
| 9157b909b12549b4a9b5aa96def27b64 | aodh                 | admin            | service |
| 4d8379b0b7d04ece973b51b2da229bc1 | glance               | admin            | service |
| 99009ed5f9374087b4300b39d36106aa | nova                 | admin            | service |
| 861bbfbcce3e48e69981f8091f04bb03 | ceilometer           | admin            | service |
| 332cd31223e8401a82a4389a1e6ef5e3 | magnum               | admin            | service |
| 9ddf79e9ce48422692568e8b93646a4c | sahara               | admin            | service |
+----------------------------------+----------------------+------------------+---------+
14 rows in set (0.00 sec)

MariaDB [keystone]>
```

Project report

Having a clear view of what project(s) exist within your cloud and the resources being used can be very valuable throughout the overall cloud lifecycle. Doing department or division chargebacks seems to be a very popular approach in recent days. Pulling these metrics as a point-in-time resources review can provide clarity around how many resources each project is using. To successfully accomplish this, the vCPU, memory, and disk metrics must be collected for each project. Using the following simple database query, you can very easily attain this information:

```
USE nova;
SELECT SUM(instances.vcpus) as vCPU, SUM(instances.memory_mb) as memory_MB,
SUM(instances.root_gb) as disk_GB, keystone.project.name as tenant from
instances
INNER JOIN keystone.project ON
instances.project_id=keystone.project.id
WHERE instances.vm_state='active' GROUP BY tenant;
```

This query will combine data from two different tables that live within two separate databases, `nova` and `keystone`. The `nova` database is the owner of all the instance-related data. The `keystone` database was reviewed in the earlier section. Just as in the previous example, each table has at least one primary key. Here is a quick breakdown of the tables used here and their functions:

```
nova
Instances # contains the raw information about instances created

keystone
Project  # contains the list of projects/tenants created/available
```

In order to attain this data, we had to get a bit crafty and pull the resource metrics directly from the table containing the raw instance information. If we had Ceilometer installed, there would be a specific database where these metrics were recorded on a much more micro level. Since we do not have this functionality available at the present time, this method is the best thing available. In this query, we will again only return the necessary columns and rename column labels. In the end, we will narrow down the output to include only active instances and sort the data by the project name in ascending order. So, by pulling the resource information about each instance and correlating it to each project where the instance belongs, we are able to create simple output similar to this:

```
+-------+-----------+---------+---------+
| vCPU  | memory_MB | disk_GB | tenant  |
+-------+-----------+---------+---------+
|     2 |      4000 |      40 | admin   |
|     3 |      6000 |      60 | tenantA |
+-------+-----------+---------+---------+
2 rows in set (0.00 sec)

MariaDB [nova]>
```

Network report

Having a snapshot of the Neutron networks created on your cloud may not seem critical to managing your overall OpenStack cloud. Trust me in the big picture it is. Unnecessary or incorrectly configured networks could add latency to overall cloud functionality. It is not the network directly that could cause this, but rather the security groups related to each project(s) network existing. This information can mainly aid in troubleshooting project-reported issues. It provides a quick reference as to what networks exist within what project and the network **Classless Inter-Domain Routing (CIDR)** aka network address space associated. Natively, the networking service (Neutron) within one command does not provide such a report. Just as earlier, we will pull this information directly from the database. Using the following simple database query, we will collect the network ID, name, subnet, CIDR assigned, status, and associated project:

```
USE neutron;
SELECT networks.id, networks.name, subnets.name as subnet, subnets.cidr,
networks.status, keystone.project.name as tenant from networks
INNER JOIN keystone.project ON networks.project_id COLLATE utf8_unicode_ci
= keystone.project.id
INNER JOIN subnets ON networks.id=subnets.network_id
ORDER BY tenant;
```

For this query, we will combine data from three different tables that live within two separate databases, `neutron` and `keystone`. The `neutron` database is the owner of all the network-related data. Here is a quick breakdown of the tables used here and their functions:

```
neutron
Networks  # contains the raw information about networks created
Subnets   # contains the subnet details associated with the networks

keystone
Project   # contains the list of projects/tenants created/available
```

[157]

Collecting these metrics was rather straightforward because most of the data existed within the networks table. All we had to do is pull in the matching CIDR taken from the subnet table and then bring in the project name associated with that network. While putting this query together, I noticed that there was an issue joining the `keystone` and `neutron` database tables. Apparently, the `neutron` database defined the schema for the ID column differently, and the following value had to be added to the inner join statement: `COLLATE utf8_unicode_ci`. In the end, the output will be sorted by the project names in ascending order. An example of the output will look similar to this:

```
+-------------------------------------+-----------------+-----------------------+----------------+--------+--------+
| id                                  | name            | subnet                | cidr           | status | tenant |
+-------------------------------------+-----------------+-----------------------+----------------+--------+--------+
| 07b3cdaa-8305-4c61-8f7e-6ca0e3f5cdbc | private-network | subnet-private-network | 10.1.100.0/24  | ACTIVE | admin  |
+-------------------------------------+-----------------+-----------------------+----------------+--------+--------+
1 row in set (0.00 sec)

MariaDB [neutron]>
```

Volume report

The capability to have detailed reports on the overall volume consumption within the cloud seems to be rather a big gap currently within OpenStack. The Block Storage service (Cinder) is responsible for maintaining and tracking the volumes within the cloud. To get accurate metrics, we would need to query Cinder directly. It would be nice to have a report to breakdown the number of volumes created per project. Then, be able to have a quick roll-up report to show how much volume storage each project is using. Now since Cinder supports multiple storage backends, you would be best to keep track of the volume type consumption as well. As Cinder matures, I am sure that this will become an easier task, but for now, we can again query the database directly to pull out the metrics we are seeking. The following are examples of the database queries used to collect these metrics:

```
USE cinder;
SELECT volumes.id, volumes.display_name as volume_name, volumes.size as
size_GB, volume_types.name as volume_type, keystone.project.name as tenant
from volumes
INNER JOIN keystone.project ON volumes.project_id=keystone.project.id
INNER JOIN volume_types ON volumes.volume_type_id=volume_types.id
WHERE volumes.status='available'
ORDER BY tenant;

SELECT SUM(volumes.size) as volume_usage_GB, keystone.project.name as
tenant from volumes
INNER JOIN keystone.project ON volumes.project_id=keystone.project.id
WHERE volumes.status='available'
```

```
GROUP BY tenant;

SELECT volume_types.name as volume_type, SUM(volumes.size) as
volume_usage_GB from volumes
INNER JOIN volume_types ON volumes.volume_type_id=volume_types.id
WHERE volumes.status='available'
GROUP BY volume_type;
```

For this query, at least three separate tables were involved with two databases, `cinder` and `keystone`. As you can see, collecting this information was quite involved. It required us to issue three separate `SELECT` statements. The first `SELECT` statement will correlate the raw volume information from the volumes table with the project data from the keystone table. Also, within this same statement, we will include the name of the volume type. Since the volumes table contains both active and inactive volumes, there had to be an additional filter applied to return only the active volumes. The complete output will then be sorted by the project name in ascending order. The output for the first query will look similar to this:

```
+----------------------------------------+-------------+---------+-------------+---------+
| id                                     | volume_name | size_GB | volume_type | tenant  |
+----------------------------------------+-------------+---------+-------------+---------+
| 03a5c760-3a82-4b80-b7b0-1062ba13fd9c   | testH       |      15 | lvm         | tenantA |
| 3fec0f0d-30f3-4d3c-95ce-cd3de4a2a5db   | testG       |      20 | lvm         | tenantA |
| fa89f9ea-7123-42cd-b8b5-07f81bc44100   | testK       |      25 | lvm         | tenantB |
+----------------------------------------+-------------+---------+-------------+---------+
3 rows in set (0.00 sec)
```

The next `SELECT` statement will query the database to collect the metrics for the total volume consumption per project. It is very similar to the previous statement, but the main difference here is we are going to add the `volume_usage_GB` column together for each project to calculate the total consumption amounts. The output for the second query will look similar to this:

```
MariaDB [cinder]>
MariaDB [cinder]> SELECT SUM(volumes.size) as volume_usage_GB, keystone.project.name as tenant from volumes
    -> INNER JOIN keystone.project ON volumes.project_id=keystone.project.id
    -> WHERE volumes.status='available'
    -> GROUP BY tenant;
+-----------------+---------+
| volume_usage_GB | tenant  |
+-----------------+---------+
|              35 | tenantA |
|              25 | tenantB |
+-----------------+---------+
2 rows in set (0.00 sec)
```

The final `SELECT` statement focuses on reporting the volume type consumption. Since the volume's table only records the volume type ID, we had to inner join the `volume_types` table to pull in the actual volume name defined when created. This was something also done for the other previously mentioned statements. The output for the third query will look similar to this:

```
MariaDB [cinder]>
MariaDB [cinder]> SELECT volume_types.name as volume_type, SUM(volumes.size) as volume_usage_GB from volumes
    -> INNER JOIN volume_types ON volumes.volume_type_id=volume_types.id
    -> WHERE volumes.status='available'
    -> GROUP BY volume_type;
+-------------+-----------------+
| volume_type | volume_usage_GB |
+-------------+-----------------+
| lvm         |              60 |
+-------------+-----------------+
1 row in set (0.01 sec)

MariaDB [cinder]>
```

Cloud-at-a-Glance report

This report is meant to be a very quick snapshot of the clouds overall consumption. It pulls back the total number of users, projects, volumes, and networks existing within your cloud. As well as, the total number of vCPU, memory, and ephemeral disk currently used. Here are the database queries used to collect this data:

```
USE keystone;
SELECT count(*) as total_users from user WHERE user.enabled=1;
SELECT count(*) as total_projects from project WHERE project.enabled=1;
USE cinder;
SELECT count(*) as total_volumes, SUM(volumes.size) as
total_volume_usage_GB from volumes
WHERE volumes.status='available';
USE neutron;
SELECT count(*) as total_networks from networks WHERE
networks.status='ACTIVE';
USE nova;
SELECT SUM(instances.vcpus) as total_vCPU, SUM(instances.memory_mb) as
total_memory_MB, SUM(instances.root_gb) as total_disk_GB from instances
WHERE instances.vm_state='active';
```

The `SELECT` statements used basically add together the columns from the table being called. The column name is then renamed to a more descriptive label and finally filtered to ignore any rows not in an active state. Once executed, the output of the preceding queries will look similar to this:

```
Database changed
MariaDB [keystone]> USE keystone;
Database changed
MariaDB [keystone]> SELECT count(*) as total_users from user WHERE user.enabled=1;
+-------------+
| total_users |
+-------------+
|          13 |
+-------------+
1 row in set (0.00 sec)

MariaDB [keystone]> SELECT count(*) as total_projects from project WHERE project.enabled=1;
+----------------+
| total_projects |
+----------------+
|              8 |
+----------------+
1 row in set (0.00 sec)

MariaDB [keystone]> USE cinder;
Reading table information for completion of table and column names
You can turn off this feature to get a quicker startup with -A

Database changed
MariaDB [cinder]> SELECT count(*) as total_volumes, SUM(volumes.size) as total_volume_usage_GB from volumes
    -> WHERE volumes.status='available';
+---------------+-----------------------+
| total_volumes | total_volume_usage_GB |
+---------------+-----------------------+
|             1 |                    10 |
+---------------+-----------------------+
1 row in set (0.00 sec)

MariaDB [cinder]> USE neutron;
Reading table information for completion of table and column names
You can turn off this feature to get a quicker startup with -A

Database changed
MariaDB [neutron]> SELECT count(*) as total_networks from networks WHERE networks.status='ACTIVE';
+----------------+
| total_networks |
+----------------+
|              1 |
+----------------+
1 row in set (0.00 sec)

MariaDB [neutron]> USE nova;
Reading table information for completion of table and column names
You can turn off this feature to get a quicker startup with -A

Database changed
MariaDB [nova]> SELECT SUM(instances.vcpus) as total_vCPU, SUM(instances.memory_mb) as total_memory_MB, SUM(instances.root_gb) as total_disk_GB from instances
    -> WHERE instances.vm_state='active';
+------------+-----------------+---------------+
| total_vCPU | total_memory_MB | total_disk_GB |
+------------+-----------------+---------------+
|          5 |           10000 |           100 |
+------------+-----------------+---------------+
1 row in set (0.00 sec)

MariaDB [nova]>
```

Now that we know how to collect the metrics for our reports, let's go and learn how we can automate this task completely.

Coding the playbook and roles

In this section, we will now create the playbook and roles to generate a comprehensive *Cloud Report*. Once the playbook is executed, the output and end result will be two reports consisting of the information we learned how to collect in the previous section. These two reports will be saved into a directory determined by you for retrieval. At that point, you can literally send it to leadership and/or peers for review. In the next chapter, we will learn how you can take things further and directly e-mail out the report as an added bonus.

Very similar to the previous chapter, we will break up the multiple tasks into separate roles to keep things organized. We will next review the six roles used to automate creating our Cloud Report.

cloud-inventory

The first role we will create will include those tasks needed to set up the foundation for the cloud report. The name of the file will be `main.yml` located within the role directory named `cloud-inventory/tasks`. The contents of this file will look like this:

```
---
  name: Create working directory
  file: path="{{ REPORT_DIR }}" state=directory
  ignore_errors: yes

  name: Copy the cloud_report script
  copy: src=cloud_report.sql dest=/usr/share mode=0755

  name: Add report header
  shell: ( echo "+-----------------------------------+"; echo "| {{ COMPANY
  }} Cloud Report     |"; echo "| Created at {{ lookup('pipe', 'date +%Y-%m-
  %d%t%X') }} |"; echo "+-----------------------------------+"; ) >> {{
  REPORT_DIR }}/os_report_{{ lookup('pipe', 'date +%Y%m%d') }}.log

  name: Execute cloud report
  shell: chdir=/usr/bin mysql -u root --password={{ MYSQLPASS }} --table <
  /usr/share/cloud_report.sql >> {{ REPORT_DIR }}/os_report_{{ lookup('pipe',
  'date +%Y%m%d') }}.log
```

The first three tasks are simply handling the prerequisite steps needed to create the report. This would include creating the directory where the report is saved, coping with the SQL script to be executed, and adding the header to the report. The overall idea is to create a visually appealing, accurate, and flexible report. This is accomplished by adding the report run time/date dynamically and naming the report accordingly. The final task will execute the `cloud_report.sql` file directly against the MySQL databases found in the Galera container of your cloud.

The `cloud_report.sql` file contains the SQL query described in the **Cloud-at-a-Glance** Report section earlier. This file can be found within the `cloud-inventory/files` directory of this role.

cloud-usage

The next role in the line-up will create the second report that will outline the current cloud utilization broken down per project. The file will be named `main.yml` located within the role directory named `cloud-usage/tasks`. The contents of this file will look like this:

```
---
 name: Create working directory
 file: path="{{ REPORT_DIR }}" state=directory
 ignore_errors: yes

 name: Retrieve projectIDs
 shell: openstack --os-cloud="{{ CLOUD_NAME }}"
     project list | awk 'NR > 3 { print $2 }'
register: tenantid

 name: Add report header
 shell: ( echo "+------------------------------------+"; echo "| Project
Usage Report         |"; echo "| Created at {{ lookup('pipe', 'date +%Y-%m-
%d%t%X') }} |"; echo "+------------------------------------+"; echo " "; )
>> {{ REPORT_DIR }}/os_usage_report_{{ lookup('pipe', 'date +%Y%m%d')
}}.log

 name: Record project usage
 shell: ( echo "Project - {{ item }}" && openstack --os-cloud="{{
CLOUD_NAME }}"
     usage show --start {{ RPTSTART }} --end {{ RPTEND }} --project {{ item
}} && echo " " ) >> {{ REPORT_DIR }}/os_usage_report_{{ lookup('pipe',
'date +%Y%m%d') }}.log
 with_items: "{{ tenantid.stdout_lines }}"

 name: Retrieve project usage report file
```

```
fetch: src={{ REPORT_DIR }}/os_usage_report_{{ lookup('pipe', 'date
+%Y%m%d') }}.log dest={{ REPORT_DEST }} flat=yes
```

All the report pre-setup work is being handled in the first and third task shown earlier (creating the report directory and header). To gather the metrics we needed for this report, we can use native OpenStack CLI commands. The two commands used are: `openstack project list` and `usage show`. These commands are executed as part of the second and fourth tasks shown above. The last task in this role will retrieve the report from the remote location and move it locally to where the playbook/roles are executed.

user-inventory

This role will be responsible for executing **User Report** described in the earlier section. The file will be named `main.yml` within the role directory name `user-inventory/tasks`. Here, you will find the contents of this file:

```
---
name: Create working directory
file: path={{ REPORT_DIR }} state=directory
ignore_errors: yes

name: Copy the user_report script
copy: src=user_report.sql dest=/usr/share mode=0755

name: Add report header
shell: ( echo "+------------------------+"; echo "| Cloud User Report
|"; echo "+------------------------+"; ) >> {{ REPORT_DIR }}/os_report_{{
lookup('pipe', 'date +%Y%m%d') }}.log

name: Execute user report
shell: chdir=/usr/bin mysql -u root --password={{ MYSQLPASS }} --table <
/usr/share/user_report.sql >> {{ REPORT_DIR }}/os_report_{{ lookup('pipe',
'date +%Y%m%d') }}.log
```

In an attempt to make the reports modular and not dependent on each other, I had each role create a report working directory and inserted report-specific headers. This way, you can include or exclude whichever roles/reports you wish.

The basic principle used to create this role will be repeated for the remaining roles. It consists of the following steps:

- Create the report working directory; if the directory already exists, it will continue reporting no error
- Copy the SQL script to the remote location

- Add custom header information to the report
- Execute the SQL script to generate the specific subreport

The user_report.sql file contains the SQL query described in the earlier section covering the **User Report**. Now that we have the framework defined, we can move quickly through the remaining roles.

project-inventory

The purpose of this role is to execute the **Project Report** we reviewed in the earlier section. The file will be named main.yml within the role directory named project-inventory/tasks. Here, you will find the contents of this file:

```
---
name: Create working directory
file: path={{ REPORT_DIR }} state=directory
ignore_errors: yes

name: Copy the tenant_report script
copy: src=project_report.sql dest=/usr/share mode=0755

name: Add report header
shell: ( echo "+-------------------------+"; echo "| Cloud Project Report
|"; echo "+-------------------------+"; ) >> {{ REPORT_DIR }}/os_report_{{
lookup('pipe', 'date +%Y%m%d') }}.log

name: Execute tenant report
 shell: chdir=/usr/bin mysql -u root --password={{ MYSQLPASS }} --table <
/usr/share/project_report.sql >> {{ REPORT_DIR }}/os_report_{{
lookup('pipe', 'date +%Y%m%d') }}.log
```

Since this role will follow the same steps outlined for the user-inventory role, we will draw attention to the unique function executed. For this role, the project_report.sql file will contain the SQL query described in the **Project Report** section earlier.

network-inventory

The purpose of this role is to execute the **Network Report** we reviewed in the earlier section. The file will be named main.yml within the role directory named network-inventory/tasks. Here, you will find the contents of this file:

```
---
```

```
name: Create working directory
file: path={{ REPORT_DIR }} state=directory
ignore_errors: yes

name: Copy the network_report script
copy: src=network_report.sql dest=/usr/share mode=0755

name: Add report header
shell: ( echo "+-------------------------+"; echo "| Cloud Network Report
|"; echo "+-------------------------+"; ) >> {{ REPORT_DIR }}/os_report_{{
lookup('pipe', 'date +%Y%m%d') }}.log

name: Execute network report
shell: chdir=/usr/bin mysql -u root --password={{ MYSQLPASS }} --table <
/usr/share/network_report.sql >> {{ REPORT_DIR }}/os_report_{{
lookup('pipe', 'date +%Y%m%d') }}.log
```

volume-inventory

This last role will execute the final subreport, which is the **Volume Report** we covered earlier. The file will be named `main.yml` within the role directory named `volume-inventory/tasks`. Here, you will find the contents of this file:

```
---
name: Create working directory
file: path={{ REPORT_DIR }} state=directory
ignore_errors: yes

name: Copy the volume_report script
copy: src=volume_report.sql dest=/usr/share mode=0755

name: Add report header
shell: ( echo "+-------------------------+"; echo "| Cloud Volume Report
|"; echo "+-------------------------+"; ) >> {{ REPORT_DIR }}/os_report_{{
lookup('pipe', 'date +%Y%m%d') }}.log

name: Execute volume report
shell: chdir=/usr/bin mysql -u root --password={{ MYSQLPASS }} --table <
/usr/share/volume_report.sql >> {{ REPORT_DIR }}/os_report_{{
lookup('pipe', 'date +%Y%m%d') }}.log

name: Retrieve completed cloud report file
fetch: src={{ REPORT_DIR }}/os_report_{{ lookup('pipe', 'date +%Y%m%d')
}}.log dest={{ REPORT_DEST }} flat=yes
```

One special thing worth noting for this role is the last task uses the `fetch` Ansible module to retrieve the report created from the remote location where it was created. This is the same behavior used in the cloud-usage role. Personally, I thought this module was very convenient and kept us from having to handle a series of secure copy commands. That is never a good time for anyone.

To support these roles, we now need to create the variable files that will go along with it. Since we will use two separate hosts to execute the series of roles against, there will be two global variable files needed. The file names are `util_container` and `galera_container`, and they will be saved to the `group_vars/` directory of the playbook.

Keep in mind that the values defined in the variable file are intended to be changed before each execution for normal everyday use.

You should note a few new variables that were defined for the new roles. Among the standard variables needed to authenticate into your OpenStack cloud, we have added some new variables related to the report creation and location:

```
util_container

# Here are variables related globally to the util_container host group

CLOUD_NAME: default

REPORT_DIR: /usr/share/os-report
REPORT_DEST: /usr/share/
RPTSTART: 2016-10-01
RPTEND: 2016-11-01

galera_container

# Here are variables related globally to the galera_container host group

MYSQLPASS: passwd
COMPANY: Rackspace RPC
REPORT_DIR: /usr/share/os-report
REPORT_DEST: /usr/share/
```

Word of caution: Due to the contents of this file, it should be stored as a secure file within whatever code repository you may use to store your Ansible playbooks/roles. Gaining access to this information could compromise your OpenStack cloud security.

Let's take a moment to break down the new variables. The summary is:

```
REPORT_DIR   # the directory where the report is
               stored temporarily remotely
REPORT_DEST  # the directory where the report is saved locally

RPTSTART     # the start date when collecting cloud usage

RPTEND       # the end date when collecting cloud usage

MYSQLPASS    # the password for the root database user

COMPANY      # the company name to show up in the report header
```

 Since there are two global variable files that share the same variable names, please make sure to keep the variable value in sync if you want both reports in the same directory. This is not a requirement, as each report (Cloud Report and Cloud Usage) can exist independently. Just felt like it was worth mentioning as to not to cause confusion.

With the variable file completed, we can move on to creating the master playbook file. Since our goal is to create one report on the clouds resources (remember that we added the Cloud Usage report as a bonus), we will call all the roles from one playbook. The complete contents of the playbook file will end up looking similar to this:

```
---
# This playbook used to run a cloud resource inventory report.

  hosts: galera_container
  remote_user: root
  become: true
  roles:
   - cloud-inventory

  hosts: util_container
  remote_user: root
  become: true
  roles:
   - cloud-usage

  hosts: galera_container
  remote_user: root
  become: true
  roles:
   - user-inventory
   - project-inventory
   - network-inventory
```

```
- volume-inventory
```

As mentioned, all the roles we created to inventory the cloud will be executed in the order displayed in the playbook. All the roles use the same host with the exception of the cloud-usage role. The reason behind this is that we used OpenStack CLI commands in that role and that then required the use of the `util_container`.

> The playbook and role names can be anything you choose. Specific names have been provided here in order to allow you to easily follow along and reference the completed code found in the GitHub repository. The only warning is that whatever you decide to name the roles, it must remain uniform when referenced from within the playbook(s).

So since we now have one additional host involved in this playbook, we must add this host to your inventory file named `hosts`. With adding the new host placeholder, the host file will now look like this example:

```
[localhost]
localhost ansible_connection=local

[util_container]
172.29.236.85

[galera_container]
172.29.236.72
```

I am extremely excited to confirm that we are now ready to start running some cloud reports. In keeping with our tradition, we will finish up the chapter with a quick review of the playbook and role just created.

Reviewing playbooks and roles

Let's jump right into examining the roles we created.

The completed role and file named `main.yml` located in the `cloud-inventory/tasks` directory looks like this:

```
---
name: Create working directory
file: path="{{ REPORT_DIR }}" state=directory
ignore_errors: yes

name: Copy the cloud_report script
copy: src=cloud_report.sql dest=/usr/share mode=0755
```

```
name: Add report header
shell: ( echo "+------------------------------------+"; echo "| {{ COMPANY
}} Cloud Report      |"; echo "| Created at {{ lookup('pipe', 'date +%Y-%m-
%d&t%X') }} |"; echo "+------------------------------------+"; ) >> {{
REPORT_DIR }}/os_report_{{ lookup('pipe', 'date +%Y%m%d') }}.log

name: Execute cloud report
shell: chdir=/usr/bin mysql -u root --password={{ MYSQLPASS }} --table <
/usr/share/cloud_report.sql >> {{ REPORT_DIR }}/os_report_{{ lookup('pipe',
'date +%Y%m%d') }}.log
```

The completed role and file named `main.yml` located in the `cloud-usage/tasks` directory
looks like this:

```
---
name: Create working directory
file: path="{{ REPORT_DIR }}" state=directory
ignore_errors: yes
name: Retrieve projectIDs
shell: openstack --os-cloud="{{ CLOUD_NAME }}"
      project list | awk 'NR > 3 { print $2 }'
register: tenantid

name: Add report header
shell: ( echo "+------------------------------------+"; echo "| Project
Usage Report       |"; echo "| Created at {{ lookup('pipe', 'date +%Y-%m-
%d&t%X') }} |"; echo "+------------------------------------+"; echo " "; )
>> {{ REPORT_DIR }}/os_usage_report_{{ lookup('pipe', 'date +%Y%m%d')
}}.log

name: Record project usage
 shell: ( echo "Project - {{ item }}" && openstack --os-cloud="{{
CLOUD_NAME }}"
      usage show --start {{ RPTSTART }} --end {{ RPTEND }} --project {{ item
}} && echo " " ) >> {{ REPORT_DIR }}/os_usage_report_{{ lookup('pipe',
'date +%Y%m%d') }}.log
 with_items: "{{ tenantid.stdout_lines }}"

name: Retrieve project usage report file
 fetch: src={{ REPORT_DIR }}/os_usage_report_{{ lookup('pipe', 'date
+%Y%m%d') }}.log dest={{ REPORT_DEST }} flat=yes
```

The completed role and file named `main.yml` located in the `user-inventory/tasks`
directory looks like this:

```
---
name: Create working directory
file: path={{ REPORT_DIR }} state=directory
```

```
ignore_errors: yes

name: Copy the user_report script
copy: src=user_report.sql dest=/usr/share mode=0755

name: Add report header
shell: ( echo "+------------------------+"; echo "| Cloud User Report
|"; echo "+------------------------+"; ) >> {{ REPORT_DIR }}/os_report_{{
lookup('pipe', 'date +%Y%m%d') }}.log

name: Execute user report
shell: chdir=/usr/bin mysql -u root --password={{ MYSQLPASS }} --table <
/usr/share/user_report.sql >> {{ REPORT_DIR }}/os_report_{{ lookup('pipe',
'date +%Y%m%d') }}.log
```

The completed role and file named `main.yml` located in the `project-inventory/tasks` directory looks like this:

```
---
name: Create working directory
file: path={{ REPORT_DIR }} state=directory
ignore_errors: yes

name: Copy the tenant_report script
copy: src=project_report.sql dest=/usr/share mode=0755
name: Add report header
shell: ( echo "+------------------------+"; echo "| Cloud Project Report
|"; echo "+------------------------+"; ) >> {{ REPORT_DIR }}/os_report_{{
lookup('pipe', 'date +%Y%m%d') }}.log

name: Execute tenant report
shell: chdir=/usr/bin mysql -u root --password={{ MYSQLPASS }} --table <
/usr/share/project_report.sql >> {{ REPORT_DIR }}/os_report_{{
lookup('pipe', 'date +%Y%m%d') }}.log
```

The completed role and file named `main.yml` located in the `network-inventory/tasks` directory looks like this:

```
---
name: Create working directory
file: path={{ REPORT_DIR }} state=directory
ignore_errors: yes

name: Copy the network_report script
copy: src=network_report.sql dest=/usr/share mode=0755

name: Add report header
shell: ( echo "+------------------------+"; echo "| Cloud Network Report
```

```
|"; echo "+------------------------+"; ) >> {{ REPORT_DIR }}/os_report_{{
lookup('pipe', 'date +%Y%m%d') }}.log

 name: Execute network report
 shell: chdir=/usr/bin mysql -u root --password={{ MYSQLPASS }} --table <
/usr/share/network_report.sql >> {{ REPORT_DIR }}/os_report_{{
lookup('pipe', 'date +%Y%m%d') }}.log
```

The completed role and file named `main.yml` located in the `volume-inventory/tasks`
directory looks like this:

```
---
 name: Create working directory
 file: path={{ REPORT_DIR }} state=directory
 ignore_errors: yes
 name: Copy the volume_report script
 copy: src=volume_report.sql dest=/usr/share mode=0755

 name: Add report header
 shell: ( echo "+-------------------------+"; echo "| Cloud Volume Report
|"; echo "+-------------------------+"; ) >> {{ REPORT_DIR }}/os_report_{{
lookup('pipe', 'date +%Y%m%d') }}.log

 name: Execute volume report
 shell: chdir=/usr/bin mysql -u root --password={{ MYSQLPASS }} --table <
/usr/share/volume_report.sql >> {{ REPORT_DIR }}/os_report_{{
lookup('pipe', 'date +%Y%m%d') }}.log

 name: Retrieve completed cloud report file
 fetch: src={{ REPORT_DIR }}/os_report_{{ lookup('pipe', 'date +%Y%m%d')
}}.log dest={{ REPORT_DEST }} flat=yes
```

The corresponding global variable file is named `util_container` and is saved to the
`group_vars/` directory of the complete playbook:

```
# Here are variables related globally to the util_container host group

CLOUD_NAME: default

REPORT_DIR: /usr/share/os-report
REPORT_DEST: /usr/share/
RPTSTART: 2016-10-01
RPTEND: 2016-11-01
```

The corresponding global variable file is named `galera_container`, and it is saved to the
`group_vars/` directory of the complete playbook:

```
# Here are variables related globally to the galera_container host group
```

```
MYSQLPASS: passwd
COMPANY: Rackspace RPC
REPORT_DIR: /usr/share/os-report
REPORT_DEST: /usr/share/
```

Now the master playbook file has been created and will be located in the `root` directory of the `playbook` directory:

inventory.yml

```
---
# This playbook used to run a cloud resource inventory report.

  hosts: galera_container
  remote_user: root
  become: true
  roles:
   - cloud-inventory
  hosts: util_container
  remote_user: root
  become: true
  roles:
   - cloud-usage

  hosts: galera_container
  remote_user: root
  become: true
  roles:
   - user-inventory
   - project-inventory
   - network-inventory
   - volume-inventory
```

Finally, we created the `hosts` file, which also is located in the `root` directory of the `playbook` directory:

```
[localhost]
localhost ansible_connection=local

[util_container]
172.29.236.85

[galera_container]
172.29.236.72
```

The complete set of code can again be found in the following GitHub repository:
`https://github.com/os-admin-with-ansible/os-admin-with-ansible-v2/tree/master/cloud-inventory`.

Before we finish up this topic, we of course need to test out our work. At the end of running this playbook and roles, you will have two reports to review. Assuming that you have cloned the GitHub repository earlier, the command to test out the playbook from the Deployment node is as follows:

```
$ cd os-admin-with-ansible-v2/cloud-inventory
$ ansible-playbook -i hosts inventory.yml
```

Assuming that the playbook ran successfully and completed with no errors, you will find the two reports created in the directory you specified in the global variable file. The report should look similar to this:

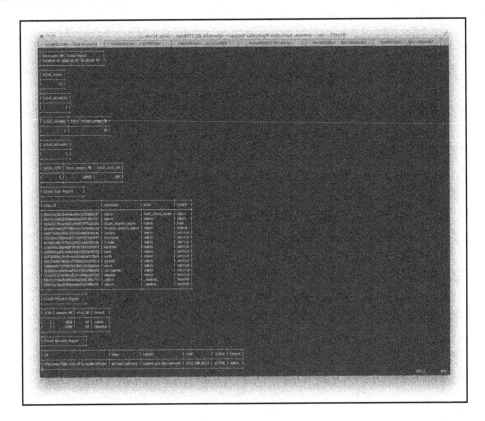

...

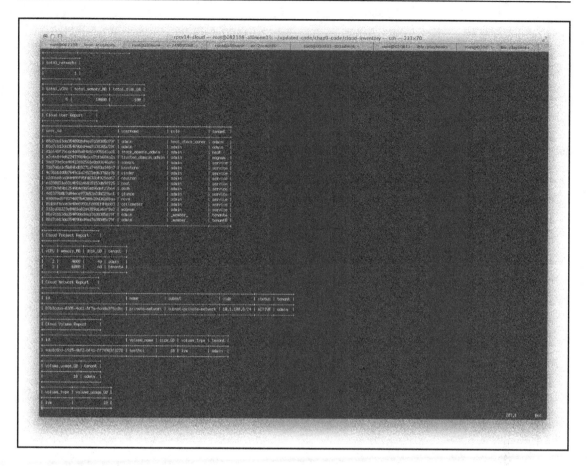

Job well done yet again! Hoping that these cloud reports can really help in simplifying your day-to-day OpenStack administrative tasks!

Summary

Our OpenStack administration toolbox is starting to look pretty full by this point in the book. Cannot stress enough how important it is to have a snapshot of your cloud state. These reports could be a good starting point to having that. Before concluding this chapter, let's take a moment to recap this chapter. Together we reviewed some gaps in OpenStack regarding reports on the clouds inventory and how you can overcome them. Then details were provided on how you can get access to the metrics and statistics we would need by querying the database. Next, we examined the custom SQL queries used to pull out the data from the database in detail. Finally, we developed Ansible playbook and role to automate generating the cloud reports.

It saddens me a bit to say that the next chapter is our last chapter. With that said, it most certainly happens to probably be one of the most important chapters. Knowing the health of your cloud is tantamount to having a working OpenStack ecosystem. Due to the modular nature of OpenStack, you will have many services to keep track of. Having them all working properly is what creates the great harmony within OpenStack. While you can certainly do it manually, I am sure that you would agree automating such a task is much more ideal. Please read on to the next chapter to learn how you can monitor the health of your cloud automatically and even have a health report delivered right to your inbox.

10

Health Check Your Cloud with Nagios

The topic of monitoring happens to be something I hold very close to my heart. I spent years *watching* many organizations' websites and applications to ensure that their availability holds as close as possible to 99.99% uptime. This task was not for the meek of heart in any realm of things. The thing that got me through it all was having a solid method to monitoring the environments that did not require me to literally watch it every second of the day. In this chapter, we will step through some of the common approaches to checking the health of your OpenStack cloud manually and then leverage Ansible to set up my favorite open source monitoring tool, Nagios.

Since we have been experimenting with the **openstack-ansible** (**OSA**) deployment method throughout the book, let's continue to leverage the built-in Ansible capabilities part of OSA to perform various system checks. Keep in mind that what we do here should not replace any third-party monitoring tool that most likely will do a better job keeping the tasks to be monitored in a reliable rotation. We will use the native capabilities part of OpenStack and Linux to provide a quick view of your clouds health. As well as along the way, we will review other monitoring tips and tricks:

- Monitoring the cloud
    - Infrastructure services
    - Core OpenStack services
- Setting up Nagios and importing checks
    - Collecting your metrics via SNMP
- Coding the playbook and roles
- Reviewing playbook and role

Monitoring the cloud

If allowed I would like to cover some monitoring basics before getting started here. Hopefully, the three principles I will share here are not new to you. When evaluating to monitor something, there are three base principles to keep in mind:

- Keep it simple
- Keep your monitoring close to your infrastructure
- Create good monitors

The first point is pretty easy to absorb, as it is rather self-explanatory. The worst thing you could ever do is over complicate something as important as monitoring. This principle not only applies to your overall approach, but it also applies to the tool you choose to do the monitoring. If you have to create a **Visio** diagram of your monitoring platform, it is too complicated.

The next point of keeping your monitoring close to your infrastructure is meant to express that the tool used to monitor should physically reside close to the infrastructure/application. The monitoring platform should not have to traverse VPNs or multiple firewalls just to poll the devices/applications. Centrally place the monitoring platform, so you can poll as many systems as possible with minimal path to travel. You should be able to open up one or two ports in a firewall to enable monitoring, and this should be turned into a standardized process part of standing up new devices/applications.

The last point is another rather self-explanatory concept. Creating good monitors is critical, and it will avoid false positive monitor alerts. Over time individuals will begin to ignore monitoring alerts if they mostly all turn out to be false alarms. Make sure that each monitoring check works as expected and is tuned to avoid false alarms as much as possible. Never launch a new alert monitor without testing it during various workloads and time of the day. Also, it should go without saying to make sure that the monitor adds value and is not redundant.

Now that we have gotten the basics out of the way, we can now focus on monitoring OpenStack. This would normally cover the following four areas:

- Monitoring the physical hardware (base resource consumption)
- Monitoring the OpenStack API endpoints
- Monitoring the OpenStack services processes
- Monitoring the Compute nodes via the infrastructure nodes

Since the first two areas are honestly better suited for a monitoring tool to handle, we will not be focusing on these tools in this book. So our focus will be primarily on checking the health of the infrastructure services (that is, Galera, RabbitMQ, and so on), the core OpenStack services processes, and the Compute nodes.

ProTip

When monitoring the OpenStack API endpoints, make sure to include the endpoint response times as a metric being recorded. This allows you to identify and track any service-related slowdowns that eventually could cause a service failure. Capturing this information allows you to see performance trends over time, which could proactively allow you to address service related issues before failures occur. The fix could be something as simple as adding more containers running that particular service, tuning service parameters, and/or database tuning.

OpenStack service processes

Before moving to the next section, I felt it would be helpful to include some details on the OpenStack service processes. Here is a table outlining the OpenStack services and the associated process names. As anything related to OpenStack, the process names are subject to change on a per release basis. I hope that this will at least be a good starting point.

Service Name	Code-Name	Process Name
Compute	Nova	nova-api-metadata, nova-api-os-compute, nova-cert, nova-compute, nova-consoleauth, nova-spicehtml5proxy, nova-api-ec2, nova-api, nova-conductor, nova-scheduler
Object Storage	Swift	swift-proxy-server, swift-account-server, swift-account-auditor, swift-account-replicator, swift-account-reaper, swift-container-server, swift-container-auditor, swift-container-replicator, swift-container-updater, swift-object-server, swift-object-auditor, swift-object-replicator, swift-object-updater
Image	Glance	glance-api, glance-registry
Identity	Keystone	keystone-all, apache2
Dashboard	Horizon	apache2
Networking	Neutron	neutron-dhcp-agent, neutron-l3-agent, neutron-linuxbridge-agent, neutron-metadata-agent, neutron-metering-agent, neutron-server

Block Storage	Cinder	cinder-api, cinder-volume, cinder-scheduler
Orchestration	Heat	heat-api, heat-api-cfn, heat-api-cloudwatch, heat-engine
Telemetry	Ceilometer	ceilometer-agent-compute, ceilometer-agent-central, ceilometer-agent-notification, ceilometer-collector, ceilometer-alarm-evaluator, ceilometer-alarm-notifier, ceilometer-api
Database	Trove	trove-api, trove-taskmanager, trove-conductor

Infrastructure services

The foundation of all the OpenStack services are called infrastructure services. These are the services/components needed just for OpenStack to work on any level. Those components are an SQL database server software, database-clustering software, and messaging server software. In our specific case, those components in the same order will be MariaDB, Galera, and RabbitMQ. Making sure that all of these components are healthy and working as expected in a top priority. Each of these software packages has native commands to report on their health, so we are covered there. So the challenge would then be what the best way to query for this information against clouds of various sizes is. Imagine that you have a 20-node control plane. You could execute the health check command twenty times or just execute one command using Ansible to get the status back.

MariaDB and Galera

Starting with the first two components, there is a way to execute one command to do both, a MySQL check as well as check the health of the database cluster. If you remember back in `Chapter 2`, *Introduction to Ansible*, we covered the topic of dynamic inventory and how OSA has prebuilt dynamic inventory scripts available that we can use to ease cloud management. We will use that capability here to streamline the process of checking on these infrastructure services.

It is useful to have a quick reminder walk through of how to use the OSA dynamic inventory scripts with Ansible. From the root OSA deployment (`/opt/openstack-ansible/playbooks`) directory, you can use the defined group names to call the containers where any of the OpenStack services reside. Each OpenStack service and infrastructure component has a group defined within the dynamic inventory. As related to the specific task we are working on presently, there is a group named `galera_container`.

This group contains all the containers where MySQL and Galera are installed for the cloud. You would then substitute this group name for any host names you would normally provide within the hosts file located inside the root directory of the playbook. Try executing the following command against your OSA cloud to reveal the details for your Galera containers:

```
$ ./inventory/dynamic_inventory.py | grep galera
```

The output will look similar to this:

```
root@021579-deploy01:/opt/os-ansible-deployment/rpc_deployment# ./inventory/dynamic_inventory.py | grep galera
    "galera_all": {
        "galera",
        "infra1_galera_container-3f1f79fb": {
            "component": "galera",
            "container_name": "infra1_galera_container-3f1f79fb",
    "galera": {
        "infra1_galera_container-3f1f79fb"
    "galera_container": {
        "infra1_galera_container-3f1f79fb"
        "infra1_galera_container-3f1f79fb",
        "infra1_galera_container-3f1f79fb",
root@021579-deploy01:/opt/os-ansible-deployment/rpc_deployment#
```

Keep in mind that the previous example was collected against an **AIO** (**All-In-One**) deployment of OpenStack. Normally, you should find three or more different containers listed under the galera_container group.

The area that we haven't covered as it relates to Ansible is the ability to issue more basic ad hoc commands using just the Ansible runtime package. Execute the following command within a command prompt where Ansible is installed to see the details on how to use the basic Ansible program:

```
$ ansible -h
```

You will note that the parameters are very similar to the ansible-playbook program with the main difference being that the ansible program is not intended to execute playbooks. Rather it is meant to be able to execute ad hoc tasks directly on the command line using all the same modules you would normally use with a playbook. We will use the basic Ansible program to demonstrate how to retrieve the status of these infrastructure services.

Now if we put this all together, the working example of reporting on the health of MySQL and Galera will look like the following:

```
$ ansible galera_container -m shell -a "mysql -h localhost\-e
  'show status like "%wsrep_cluster_%";'"
```

The preceding command told Ansible to use the `galera_container` group as the hosts to run the `shell` command against. The `shell` command will call MySQL and execute the `show status` query. The output of the command will look similar to this:

```
root@021579-deploy01:/opt/os-ansible-deployment/rpc_deployment# ansible galera_container -m shell -a "mysql -h localhost\
> -e 'show status like \"%wsrep_cluster_%\";'"
infra1_galera_container-3f1f79fb | success | rc=0 >>
Variable_name    Value
wsrep_cluster_conf_id    1
wsrep_cluster_size       1
wsrep_cluster_state_uuid       55067fd1-834d-11e5-a916-fa366d44982c
wsrep_cluster_status     Primary

root@021579-deploy01:/opt/os-ansible-deployment/rpc_deployment#
```

Again, due to using an AIO deployment, you will note that the example shows a cluster size of only one. Normally, the cluster size should show three or more, and the status will be displayed for each container (the output will be repeated for each container). Key areas to look out for are: each container reports success, the cluster size is correct, and the cluster ID is the same across all clusters.

RabbitMQ

We will use the very same principles as we did earlier for MariaDB/Galera to check on the status and health of the RabbitMQ cluster. The group name for the RabbitMQ containers is `rabbit_mq_container`, and we can see the details of the group by executing the following command within the OSA root deployment directory:

```
$./inventory/dynamic_inventory.py | greprabbit_mq
```

We can now go ahead and test out a few commands to report on the RabbitMQ cluster health. The first command here will report directly on the cluster status, and the second command will list out all the queues that contain messages (in other words queues that are not empty):

```
$ ansible rabbit_mq_container -m shell -a "rabbitmqctlcluster_status"
$ ansible rabbit_mq_container -m shell -a
  "rabbitmqctllist_queues | awk '\$2>0'"
```

The output of the commands will look similar to this:

```
root@021579-deploy01:/opt/os-ansible-deployment/rpc_deployment# ansible rabbit_mq_container -m shell -a "rabbitmqctl cluster_status"
infra1_rabbit_mq_container-6193dd22 | success | rc=0 >>
Cluster status of node 'rabbit@infra1_rabbit_mq_container-6193dd22' ...
[{nodes,[{disc,['rabbit@infra1_rabbit_mq_container-6193dd22']}]},
 {running_nodes,['rabbit@infra1_rabbit_mq_container-6193dd22']},
 {cluster_name,<<"rpc">>},
 {partitions,[]}]

root@021579-deploy01:/opt/os-ansible-deployment/rpc_deployment# ansible rabbit_mq_container -m shell -a "rabbitmqctl list_queues | awk '\$2>0'"
infra1_rabbit_mq_container-6193dd22 | success | rc=0 >>
Listing queues ...
notifications.info      34

root@021579-deploy01:/opt/os-ansible-deployment/rpc_deployment#
```

Having each container report back a *success*, having the list of running nodes match exactly and each showing the same cluster name are the areas that matter the most. Do not stress too much if you find queues with messages still present. The idea is those messages should clear in an acceptable period of time. Use this metric to seek out any trends in messages getting stuck in the queue for too long.

Core OpenStack services

With all the infrastructure services covered, we can move on to the core OpenStack services. In this section, we will cover a few principles that can be used for any of the OpenStack services. This approach allows you to interchange any of the basic approaches for any service basing it on your personal needs.

The first three services I normally go in and check are Keystone, Nova, and Neutron. These services can have adverse effects on many other services within your cloud and need to be running properly to technically have a functioning cloud. While there is no distinct OpenStack command you can use to check the Keystone service, it will become very apparently obvious if the Keystone service is not operational as any/all OpenStack CLI commands will fail. I personally find the easiest way to test our Keystone is to either log into the Horizon dashboard or issue the following OpenStack CLI command:

```
$ openstack service list
```

If you get back the list of services using Keystone, you have just tested passing user credentials to Keystone for authentication and Keystone returning a proper token for authorization. With us taking care of testing out Keystone, the next step can be to issue two OpenStack CLI commands that will quickly report on the state of Nova and Neutron:

```
$ nova service-list
$ neutron agent-list
```

The `nova service-list` command will poll all Nova-related containers and Compute nodes to determine their zone, status, state, and time either the status or state was changed. The output of this command will look similar to this:

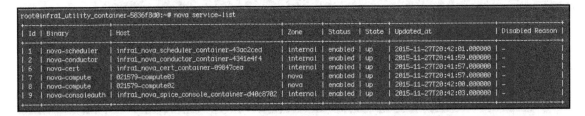

Next, the `neutron agent-list` command will do the same thing as the above except for the Neutron-related components. You will note that in the upcoming example a smiley face graphic is used to determine the status of the neutron agents. The state of the agents will also be reported back with this command as well:

```
root@infra1_utility_container-5836f8d0:~# neutron agent-list
+--------------------------------------+--------------------+------------------------------------------------+-------+----------------+---------------------------+
| id                                   | agent_type         | host                                           | alive | admin_state_up | binary                    |
+--------------------------------------+--------------------+------------------------------------------------+-------+----------------+---------------------------+
| 8316ab4e-47f1-40e1-82dd-8a78e7621e3f | Metadata agent     | infra1_neutron_agents_container-bda7cb47       | :-)   | True           | neutron-metadata-agent    |
| 8577b3b7-689f-44b3-859f-daf988897c62 | Linux bridge agent | 021579-compute02                               | :-)   | True           | neutron-linuxbridge-agent |
| 8e8adb05-43cf-4b61-a578-b01f8953ed15 | DHCP agent         | infra1_neutron_agents_container-bda7cb47       | :-)   | True           | neutron-dhcp-agent        |
| b13d81b7-4d0f-407c-b8db-11ced9056dd0 | L3 agent           | infra1_neutron_agents_container-bda7cb47       | :-)   | True           | neutron-l3-agent          |
| dd5d1262-0599-45a9-b8d3-1ec3d3078c15 | Linux bridge agent | 021579-compute03                               | :-)   | True           | neutron-linuxbridge-agent |
| e71d6f61-acbb-4fb6-9f8d-d16f59597c66 | Metering agent     | infra1_neutron_agents_container-bda7cb47       | :-)   | True           | neutron-metering-agent    |
| f40c9ece-ebbb-4624-a4bd-5d1a61794e5b | Linux bridge agent | infra1_neutron_agents_container-bda7cb47       | :-)   | True           | neutron-linuxbridge-agent |
+--------------------------------------+--------------------+------------------------------------------------+-------+----------------+---------------------------+
```

At this point, you will have to rely on checking directly on the statuses of the actual OpenStack service processes running within their containers to do more detailed monitoring. This would be similar to some of the methods published on the OpenStack website, http://docs.openstack.org/ops-guide/operations.html. The main difference is that we will use Ansible to execute the commands across all containers or nodes as needed. Using the basic Ansible program and the OpenStack service processes table mentioned previously, you will be able to check the status of the processes running OpenStack within your cloud. The following are a few examples of how this can be accomplished. It is recommended to get a complete output of the dynamic inventory for your cloud, so you will be aware of all the groups defined. Use the following command to get the complete inventory output (this command assumes that you are in the root OSA deployment directory):

```
$ cd playbooks/inventory
$ ./dynamic_inventory.py
```

Save the JSON output at some place where you can reference it in the future.

Service and process check examples

The following examples show that how you can execute service and process monitor checks using Ansible:

```
# check if a process is running
$ ansible neutron_server_container -m shell -a
  "ps -ef | grep neutron-server"
# check status of a service
$ ansible compute_hosts -m shell -a "service nova-compute status"
# stop/start/restart a service (process)
$ ansible glance_container -m shell -a "service glance-registry stop"
$ ansible glance_container -m shell -a "service glance-registry start"
$ ansible glance_container -m shell -a "service glance-registry restart"
# parseservice logs
$ ansible nova_scheduler_container -m shell -a
  "grep 35f83ac8 /var/log/nova/nova-scheduler.log"
```

You can use any of these examples to determine the health of your OpenStack services on a cloud of any size, big or small. Imagine that the power of being able to query the `nova-compute` service status across a cloud with 200 nodes in one command. Good stuff right? Well, of course, we have to try to take it to the next level by incorporating more advance monitoring tools into the mix to create a more robust solution.

Setting up Nagios and import checks

Reflecting back to the first principle mentioned previously concerning monitoring, keep it simple. It felt like we could not keep it any simpler than going with one of the leading open source monitoring platforms, Nagios Core. If you are unfamiliar with Nagios, take a moment to read up on it by visiting `http://www.nagios.com/products`.

Yes, yes, while it may not be the flashiest dashboard visually, it is one of the most powerful and lightweight monitoring applications I have used. With Nagios, you have ultimate control on many aspects of your monitoring ecosystem. It ranges from being able to create custom plugins, all the way to explicitly defining execution windows for that host. Administration can be handled directly from the flat files, or you can use many of the third-party tools, such as **NConf** at `http://exchange.nagios.org/directory/Addons/Configuration/NConf/details`. With the launch of the new version, XI, more and more of the features only found in the third-party tools are built right in. Some of the new features that stand out are the advanced graphs, integration into Incident management tools, and cleaner SLA reports.

Collect your metrics via SNMP

Of course, with great capability sometimes comes great overhead. Typically, I have found that keeping your monitoring close to your infrastructure avoids limiting what you are monitoring due to firewall restrictions and so on. It is strongly recommend to use SNMP (UDP port `161`), rather than the NRPE agent, no agent installation is needed. As well as, I normally stick with Perl-written plugins to ease troubleshooting. Creating good'monitors is essential to minimize false alerts, which in time turn into ignored alerts. If you find a service check continuously sending off false alerts, FIX IT! Do not let it linger for days.

Because of the power behind OpenStack exposing all functionality through APIs, monitoring is made easy. Custom plugin scripts can be created to monitor the whole OpenStack stack and cross-reference any bottlenecks to physical infrastructure problems. This type of proactive monitoring can lead to preventing down time leading to outages.

Since I have such a deep seeded love for OSA, it seemed only fitting to put together a series of Ansible playbooks to handle most of the Nagios and NConf setup. Also, because I love to pay it forward, included are OSA customized Nagios configs (`checkcommands`, services and a bunch of global Nagios configs) which can be used to monitor your OpenStack cloud within minutes.

Coding the playbooks and roles

In this section, we will now use all of that Ansible magic to create a series of playbooks and roles to set up Nagios to monitor your OpenStack cloud. Once completed, you will have a fully functioning Nagios installation that will be customized to monitor OpenStack with some of the monitoring checks we reviewed in the previous section. This time around we broken up the tasks into eight roles in order to keep things simple. Let's review each role in the later .

snmp-config

The first role we will create will include those tasks needed to set up the foundation for collecting the monitoring data. The name of the file will be `main.yml` located within the `role` directory named `snmp-config/tasks`. The contents of this file will look like this:

```
---

  name: Install additional packages
  apt: name="{{ item }}" state=present
```

```
with_items:
- snmpd

name: Move standard config
command: mv /etc/snmp/snmpd.conf /etc/snmp/snmpd.conf.org

name: Place new config file
template: src=snmpd.conf dest=/etc/snmp/snmpd.conf

name: Update SNMP options
shell: chdir=/bin sed -i 's+^SNMPDOPTS.*+SNMPDOPTS="-Lsd -Lf /dev/null -u
snmp -I -smux -p /var/run/snmpd.pid -c /etc/snmp/snmpd.conf"+'
/etc/default/snmpd

name: Stop SNMP service
command: service snmpd stop

name: Start SNMP service
command: service snmpd start

name: Set SNMP service to start automatically
command: update-rc.d snmpd defaults
```

The first four tasks are simply handling the steps needed to install and configure SNMP on each host you will be monitoring. This will include installing the `snmp` package, copying the custom config file into place, and editing the SNMP options.

The task handling the custom `snmp.conf` will use a `template` file stored in the `snmp-config/templates` directory of this role. The reason for this is so we can leverage the variables defined in your playbook already instead of hard coding parameters. The contents of the file will look like this:

```
rocommunity {{ SNMP_COMMUNITY }}
syslocation {{ SYS_LOCATION }}
syscontact {{ SYS_CONTACT }}
```

install-nagios

The next role will focus on installing Nagios and its prerequisites. The file will be named `main.yml` located within the `role` directory named `install-nagios/tasks`. The contents of this file will look like this:

```
---

name: Install additional packages
```

```
    apt: name={{item}} state=present
    with_items:
    - vim
     - nagios3
     - unzip

    name: Backup Nagios config files
    command: cp -r /etc/nagios3 /etc/nagios3.backup

    name: Check Nagios service
    shell: ps -ef |grep nagios3

    name: Create user .ssh directory
    file: path=/var/lib/nagios/.ssh state=directory
    ignore_errors: yes

    name: Copy SSH private keys
    copy: src=id_dsa dest=/var/lib/nagios/.ssh mode=0600
    name: Copy SSH public keys
    copy: src=id_dsa.pub dest=/var/lib/nagios/.ssh mode=0644
    name: Copy nagios Ubuntu logo archive
    copy: src=nagios-ubuntu-logo.tar dest=/usr/share
    name: Decompress nagios Ubuntu logo archive
    command: chdir=/usr/share tar xvf nagios-ubuntu-logo.tar -C
/usr/share/nagios/htdocs/images/logos/base
```

This role is pretty straightforward in stepping through the tasks needed to perform a clean installation of Nagios. Since we will be monitoring Ubuntu systems, the last two tasks in this role were included for install the Ubuntu logo into Nagios.

nagios-plugins

This role will be responsible for installing our custom Nagios plugins that we will use to monitor our cloud. The file will be named `main.yml` within the `role` directory named `nagios-plugins/tasks`. Here, you will find these contents:

```
    ---

    name: Copy nagios plugins tar file
    copy: src=nagios-plugins.tar dest=/usr/share

    name: Decompress nagios plugins archive
    command: chdir=/usr/share tar xvf nagios-plugins.tar -C
/usr/lib/nagios/plugins

    name: Confirm plugin file permissions
```

```
file: path=/usr/lib/nagios/plugins/* mode=0774

name: Confirm plugin file ownership
file: path=/usr/lib/nagios/plugins owner=nagios owner=nagios recurse=yes
name: Copy nagios configs zip file
copy: src=NagiosConfig.zip dest=/usr/share

- name: Create rpc-nagios-configs directory
  file: path=/etc/nagios3/rpc-nagios-configs state=directory

name: Decompress nagios configs archive
command: chdir=/usr/share unzip NagiosConfig.zip -d /etc/nagios3/rpc-
nagios-configs
```

The preceding role copies and sets up two very important files (nagios-plugins.tar and NagiosConfig.zip) on the Nagios server. Without these plugins and configurations, you will just have a plain vanilla Nagios installation. By running this role, you basically are getting a preconfigured Nagios setup ready to monitor an OpenStack cloud deployed with OSA. With this model, you can also customize the plugins or specific configurations being attached to the Nagios server. If you are feeling curious, feel free to crack open these archives and take a look.

install-nconf

This role could technically be considered optional, as you do not need NConf to run a Nagios server. I personally have found NConf to be a great compliment to Nagios as far as configuring your service checks and hosts. The file will be named main.yml within the role directory named install-nconf/tasks. Here are the contents of this file:

```
---

name: Install additional packages
apt: name={{item}} state=present
with_items:
  - mysql-server
  - mysql-client
  - php5
  - libapache2-mod-php5
  - php5-mysql
  - php5-cli
  - php5-common
  - libtext-csv-xs-perl
name: Download NConf binaries
command: wget
http://sourceforge.net/projects/nconf/files/nconf/1.3.0-0/nconf-1.3.0-0.tgz
```

```
/download -O /usr/share/nconf-1.3.0-0.tgz

 name: Unpack NConf binaries
 command: chdir=/usr/share tar xzvf nconf-1.3.0-0.tgz -C /var/www/html
 name: Set proper NConf directory permissions
 command: chdir=/var/www/html/nconf chmod 644 config output static_cfg temp
 name: Copy NConf DB script
 template: src=create-nconf-db.sql dest=/usr/share

 name: Create NConf DB
 shell: chdir=/usr/bin mysql -u "{{ DB_USER }}" --password= <
/usr/share/create-nconf-db.sql

- name: Set NConf directory ownership
 file: path=/var/www/html/nconf owner=www-data group=www-data recurse=yes

- name: Set NConf directory permissions
 file: path=/var/www/html/nconf mode=0777

- name: Stop apache
 command: service apache2 stop
- name: Start apache
 command: service apache2 start
```

 Very similar to the role that handles installing Nagios, it covers the required steps to install and configure NConf. More details on how to install NConf can be found at `http://www.nconf.org/dokuwiki/doku.ph p?id=nconf:help:documentation:start:installation`.

nconf-post-install

Consider this role a follow-up to the previous one as it handles the post-install steps for the NConf installation. It will handle the cleanup of specific files once the install has completed. The file will be named `main.yml` within the `role` directory named `nconf-post-install/tasks`. Here are the contents of this file:

```
---

 name: Remove installation directories and files
 command: rm -r /var/www/html/nconf/INSTALL

 name: Remove installation directories and files
 command: rm /var/www/html/nconf/INSTALL.php
 name: Remove installation directories and files
 command: rm -r /var/www/html/nconf/UPDATE
```

```
name: Remove installation directories and files
command: rm /var/www/html/nconf/UPDATE.php
```

The next two roles are intended to prepare the controller nodes to monitor the OpenStack processes and API's running on the local containers. You must be able to run the service checks remotely over SSH. The good news is that the Nagios plugin to do this already exists (check_by_ssh).

create-nagios-user

The name of this role basically explains exactly what tasks it will handle. It will create a user named Nagios, and this user will serve as a service account for the Nagios plugin. The file will be named main.yml within the role directory named create-nagios-user/tasks. Here are the contents of this file:

```
---

name: Create Nagios user
user: name="{{ USER }}" comment="{{ USER }} User"
ignore_errors: yes

name: Create user .ssh directory
file: path=/home/"{{ USER }}"/.ssh state=directory

name: Copy authorized keys
copy: src=nagios-key dest=/home/"{{ USER }}"/.ssh/authorized_keys
mode=0644

name: Set home directory permissions
file: path=/home/"{{ USER }}" owner="{{ USER }}" group="{{ USER }}"
recurse=yes
```

infra-plugin-config

This role will install additional SNMP package prerequisites and install local Nagios plugins directly on the controller node. Via SSH, Nagios will execute these local plugins and report the status back to Nagios to record. This is where you have to say that you just love technology. The file will be named main.yml within the role directory named infra-plugin-config/tasks. Here are the contents of this file:

```
---

name: Install additional packages
```

```
apt: name={{item}} state=present
with_items:
 - libnet-snmp-perl
name: Create bin directory
file: path=/home/"{{ USER }}"/bin state=directory
ignore_errors: yes

name: Fix libcrypto link
command: chdir=/lib/x86_64-linux-gnu ln -s libcrypto.so.1.0.0
libcrypto.so.6
 ignore_errors: yes
name: Fix libssl link
command: chdir=/lib/x86_64-linux-gnu ln -s libssl.so.1.0.0 libssl.so.6
 ignore_errors: yes
name: Copy nagios plugins
copy: src=check_http dest=/home/"{{ USER }}"/bin
name: Copy nagios plugins
copy: src=check_port.pl dest=/home/"{{ USER }}"/bin
name: Copy nagios plugins
copy: src=check_snmp_process.pl dest=/home/"{{ USER }}"/bin
name: Copy nagios plugins
copy: src=show_users dest=/home/"{{ USER }}"/bin
name: Copy perl utils
copy: src=utils.pm dest=/etc/perl
name: Copy perl utils
copy: src=utils.sh dest=/etc/perl
name: Confirm plugin file permissions
file: path=/home/nagios/bin/check* mode=0777

name: Confirm plug file ownership
file: path=/home/nagios/bin owner=nagios group=nagios recurse=yes
```

nagios-post-install

Last and certainly not least is the final role that makes up this series. The final role will complete the Nagios configuration and set up NConf to work with your Nagios installation. The file will be named `main.yml` within the `role` directory named `nagios-post-install/tasks`. Here are the contents of this file:

```
---

name: Copy NConf config file
copy: src=nconf.php dest=/var/www/html/nconf/config mode=0644

name: Change default Nagios config to use NConf
shell: chdir=/bin sed -i 's/^cfg_dir.*/#/g' /etc/nagios3/nagios.cfg
```

```
name: Change default Nagios config to use NConf
shell: chdir=/bin sed -i 's/^cfg_file.*/#/g' /etc/nagios3/nagios.cfg

name: Make import directory
file: path=/etc/nagios3/import state=directory
name: Copy Nagios config snippet
copy: src=nagios.txt dest=/usr/share
name: Change default Nagios config to use NConf
shell: chdir=/usr/share cat /usr/share/nagios.txt >>
/etc/nagios3/nagios.cfg
name: Copy updated NConf deployment script
copy: src=deploy_local.sh dest=/var/www/html/nconf/ADD-ONS mode=0777
```

To support these roles, we now need to create the variable files that will go along with it. Since we will use three separate hosts to execute the series of roles against, there will be three global variable files needed. The file names are `hosts`, `all_containers`, and `nagios-server`; they will be saved to the `group_vars/` directory of the playbook.

> Keep in mind that the values defined in the variable file are intended to be changed before each execution for normal everyday use.

There are a bunch of new variables added in this chapter. Let's take a moment to review the contents of each variable file:

```
all_containers

# Here are variables related to the install

USER: nagios
SNMP_COMMUNITY: osad
SYS_LOCATION: SAT
SYS_CONTACT: support@rackspace.com

hosts

# Here are variables related to the install

USER: nagios
SNMP_COMMUNITY: osad
SYS_LOCATION: SAT
SYS_CONTACT: support@rackspace.com

nagios-server

# Here are variables related to the install
```

```
DB_NAME: NCONF_DB
DB_USER: root
DB_PASS: passwd
```

Let's take a moment to break down the new variables. The summary is:

```
USER              # user to be created on the OSA nodes to match up
                    against the default Nagios user created,
                    the default user is 'nagios'
SNMP_COMMUNITY # the SNMP community string used for
                    the OSA nodes and containers
SYS_LOCATION    # additional SNMP information (optional)

SYS_CONTACT     # additional SNMP information (optional)

DB_NAME         # name of the NConf database to be created

DB_USER         # root user for the local mysql server

DB_PASS         # root user password for the local mysql server
```

 Since there are two global variable files that share the same variable names, please make sure to keep the variable value in sync if you want both reports in the same directory.

With the variable file completed, we can move on to creating the master playbook file. Since there will be manual configurations that need to be taken care of inbetween the playbooks to be run, the master playbook was broken up into multiple playbooks. The contents of the first playbook named base.yml will look like this:

```
---
# This playbook deploys components needed for Infrastructure hosts and
containers.

hosts: all_containers
remote_user: root
become: true
roles:
  - snmp-config
hosts: hosts
remote_user: root
become: true
roles:
  - snmp-config
```

The next playbook is named `base-nagios.yml`, and the contents will look like this:

```
---
# This playbook deploys components needed for Nagios.

  hosts: nagios-server
  remote_user: root
  become: true
  roles:
   - install-nagios
   - nagios-plugins
```

The following playbook is named `base-nconf.yml`, and the contents will look like this:

```
---
# This playbook deploys components needed for NConf.

  hosts: nagios-server
  remote_user: root
  become: true
  roles:
   - install-nconf
```

The next playbook is named `post-nconf-install.yml`, and the contents will look like this:

```
---
# This playbook deploys components needed for NConf.

  hosts: nagios-server
  remote_user: root
  become: true
  roles:
   - nconf-post-install
```

The next playbook is named `base-infra.yml`, and the contents will look like this:

```
---
# This playbook deploys components needed for the Infrastructure hosts.
  hosts: hosts
  remote_user: root
  become: true
  roles:
   - create-nagios-user
   - infra-plugin-config
```

The next playbook is named `post-nagios-install.yml`, and the contents will look like this:

```
---
# This playbook deploys components needed for NConf.

  hosts: nagios-server
  remote_user: root
  become: true
  roles:
   - nagios-post-install
```

 The playbook and role names can be anything you choose. Specific names have been provided here in order to allow you to easily follow along and reference the completed code found in the GitHub repository. The only warning is that whatever you decide to name the roles must remain uniform when referenced from within the playbook(s).

Our inventory file for these playbooks and roles turns out to be a very simple one. Inside the inventory file, we will only have to define the address of the Nagios server. An example of this is shown as follows:

```
[nagios-server]
021579-nagios01
```

I hope that you are happy with how it all came out. In keeping with our tradition, we will finish up the chapter with a quick review of the playbooks and roles just created with a little added extra instructions included.

Reviewing playbooks and roles

Let's jump right into examining the roles we created.

The completed role and file named `main.yml` located in the `snmp-config/tasks` directory looks like this:

```
---

  name: Install additional packages
  apt: name="{{ item }}" state=present
  with_items:
   - snmpd
  name: Move standard config
  command: mv /etc/snmp/snmpd.conf /etc/snmp/snmpd.conf.org
```

```
name: Place new config file
template: src=snmpd.conf dest=/etc/snmp/snmpd.conf
name: Update SNMP options
shell: chdir=/bin sed -i 's+^SNMPDOPTS.*+SNMPDOPTS="-Lsd -Lf /dev/null -u
snmp -I -smux -p /var/run/snmpd.pid -c /etc/snmp/snmpd.conf"+'
/etc/default/snmpd

name: Stop SNMP service
command: service snmpd stop

name: Start SNMP service
command: service snmpd start
name: Set SNMP service to start automatically
command: update-rc.d snmpd defaults
```

The completed role and file named `main.yml` located in the `install-nagios/tasks` directory looks like this:

```
---

name: Install additional packages
apt: name={{item}} state=present
with_items:
 - vim
 - nagios3
 - unzip

name: Backup Nagios config files
command: cp -r /etc/nagios3 /etc/nagios3.backup
name: Check Nagios service
shell: ps -ef |grep nagios3

name: Create user .ssh directory
file: path=/var/lib/nagios/.ssh state=directory
ignore_errors: yes

name: Copy SSH private keys
copy: src=id_dsa dest=/var/lib/nagios/.ssh mode=0600
name: Copy SSH public keys
copy: src=id_dsa.pub dest=/var/lib/nagios/.ssh mode=0644
name: Copy nagios Ubuntu logo archive
copy: src=nagios-ubuntu-logo.tar dest=/usr/share
name: Decompress nagios Ubuntu logo archive
command: chdir=/usr/share tar xvf nagios-ubuntu-logo.tar -C
/usr/share/nagios/htdocs/images/logos/base
```

The completed role and file named `main.yml` located in the `nagios-plugins/tasks` directory looks like this:

```
---

name: Copy nagios plugins tar file
copy: src=nagios-plugins.tar dest=/usr/share

name: Decompress nagios plugins archive
command: chdir=/usr/share tar xvf nagios-plugins.tar -C
/usr/lib/nagios/plugins

name: Confirm plugin file permissions
file: path=/usr/lib/nagios/plugins/* mode=0774

name: Confirm plugin file ownership
file: path=/usr/lib/nagios/plugins owner=nagios owner=nagios recurse=yes
name: Copy nagios configs zip file
copy: src=NagiosConfig.zip dest=/usr/share

name: Create rpc-nagios-configs directory
file: path=/etc/nagios3/rpc-nagios-configs state=directory

name: Decompress nagios configs archive
command: chdir=/usr/share unzip NagiosConfig.zip -d /etc/nagios3/rpc-
nagios-configs
```

The completed role and file named `main.yml` located in the `install-nconf/tasks` directory looks like this:

```
---

name: Install additional packages
apt: name={{item}} state=present
with_items:
 - mysql-server
 - mysql-client
 - php5
 - libapache2-mod-php5
 - php5-mysql
 - php5-cli
 - php5-common
 - libtext-csv-xs-perl
- name: Download NConf binaries
 command: wget
http://sourceforge.net/projects/nconf/files/nconf/1.3.0-0/nconf-1.3.0-0.tgz
/download -O /usr/share/nconf-1.3.0-0.tgz
```

```
name: Unpack NConf binaries
command: chdir=/usr/share tar xzvf nconf-1.3.0-0.tgz -C /var/www/html
name: Set proper NConf directory permissions
command: chdir=/var/www/html/nconf chmod 644 config output static_cfg temp
- name: Copy NConf DB script
template: src=create-nconf-db.sql dest=/usr/share

name: Create NConf DB
shell: chdir=/usr/bin mysql -u "{{ DB_USER }}" --password= <
/usr/share/create-nconf-db.sql

- name: Set NConf directory ownership
file: path=/var/www/html/nconf owner=www-data group=www-data recurse=yes

name: Set NConf directory permissions
file: path=/var/www/html/nconf mode=0777

name: Stop apache
command: service apache2 stop
name: Start apache
command: service apache2 start
```

The completed role and file named `main.yml` located in the `nconf-post-install/tasks`
directory looks like this:

```
---

name: Remove installation directories and files
command: rm -r /var/www/html/nconf/INSTALL

name: Remove installation directories and files
command: rm /var/www/html/nconf/INSTALL.php
name: Remove installation directories and files
command: rm -r /var/www/html/nconf/UPDATE
name: Remove installation directories and files
command: rm /var/www/html/nconf/UPDATE.php
```

The completed role and file named `main.yml` located in the `create-nagios-user/tasks`
directory looks like this:

```
---

name: Create Nagios user
user: name="{{ USER }}" comment="{{ USER }} User"
ignore_errors: yes

name: Create user .ssh directory
file: path=/home/"{{ USER }}"/.ssh state=directory
```

```
name: Copy authorized keys
copy: src=nagios-key dest=/home/"{{ USER }}"/.ssh/authorized_keys
mode=0644

name: Set home directory permissions
file: path=/home/"{{ USER }}" owner="{{ USER }}" group="{{ USER }}"
recurse=yes
```

The completed role and file named `main.yml` located in the `infra-plugin-config/tasks` directory looks like this:

```
---

name: Install additional packages
apt: name={{item}} state=present
with_items:
 - libnet-snmp-perl
name: Create bin directory
file: path=/home/"{{ USER }}"/bin state=directory
ignore_errors: yes

name: Fix libcrypto link
command: chdir=/lib/x86_64-linux-gnu ln -s libcrypto.so.1.0.0
libcrypto.so.6
ignore_errors: yes
name: Fix libcrypto link
command: chdir=/lib/x86_64-linux-gnu ln -s libssl.so.1.0.0 libssl.so.6
ignore_errors: yes
name: Copy nagios plugins
copy: src=check_http dest=/home/"{{ USER }}"/bin
name: Copy nagios plugins
copy: src=check_port.pl dest=/home/"{{ USER }}"/bin
name: Copy nagios plugins
copy: src=check_snmp_process.pl dest=/home/"{{ USER }}"/bin
name: Copy nagios plugins
copy: src=show_users dest=/home/"{{ USER }}"/bin
name: Copy perl utils
copy: src=utils.pm dest=/etc/perl
name: Copy perl utils
copy: src=utils.sh dest=/etc/perl
name: Confirm plugin file permissions
file: path=/home/nagios/bin/check* mode=0777

name: Confirm plug file ownership
file: path=/home/nagios/bin owner=nagios group=nagios recurse=yes
```

The completed role and file named `main.yml` located in the `nagios-post-install/tasks` directory looks like this:

```
---

name: Copy NConf config file
copy: src=nconf.php dest=/var/www/html/nconf/config mode=0644

name: Change default Nagios config to use NConf
shell: chdir=/bin sed -i 's/^cfg_dir.*/#/g' /etc/nagios3/nagios.cfg

name: Change default Nagios config to use NConf
shell: chdir=/bin sed -i 's/^cfg_file.*/#/g' /etc/nagios3/nagios.cfg

name: Make import directory
file: path=/etc/nagios3/import state=directory
name: Copy Nagios config snippet
copy: src=nagios.txt dest=/usr/share
name: Change default Nagios config to use NConf
shell: chdir=/usr/share cat /usr/share/nagios.txt >>
/etc/nagios3/nagios.cfg
name: Copy updated NConf deployment script
copy: src=deploy_local.sh dest=/var/www/html/nconf/ADD-ONS mode=0777
```

The corresponding global variable file is named `all_containers` and is saved to the `group_vars/` directory of the complete playbook:

```
# Here are variables related to the install

USER: nagios
SNMP_COMMUNITY: osad
SYS_LOCATION: SAT
SYS_CONTACT: support@rackspace.com
```

The corresponding global variable file is named `hosts` and is saved to the `group_vars/` directory of the complete playbook:

```
# Here are variables related to the install

USER: nagios
SNMP_COMMUNITY: osad
SYS_LOCATION: SAT
SYS_CONTACT: support@rackspace.com
```

The corresponding global variable file is named `nagios-server` and is saved to the `group_vars/` directory of the complete playbook:

```
# Here are variables related to the install

DB_NAME: NCONF_DB
DB_USER: root
DB_PASS: passwd
```

Now the master playbook file has been created and will be located in the `root` directory of the `playbook` directory:

- `base.yml`

  ```
  ---
  # This playbook deploys components needed for Infrastructure hosts and
  containers.

    hosts: all_containers
    remote_user: root
    become: true
    roles:
     - snmp-config
    hosts: hosts
    remote_user: root
    become: true
    roles:
     - snmp-config
  ```

- `base-nagios.yml`

  ```
  ---
  # This playbook deploys components needed for Nagios.
   hosts: nagios-server
   remote_user: root
   become: true
   roles:
    - install-nagios
    - nagios-plugins
  ```

- `base-nconf.yml`

  ```
  ---
  # This playbook deploys components needed for NConf.

    hosts: nagios-server
  ```

```
    remote_user: root
    become: true
    roles:
     - install-nconf
```

● post-nconf-install.yml

```
    ---
    # This playbook deploys components needed for NConf.

    hosts: nagios-server
    remote_user: root
    become: true
    roles:
     - nconf-post-install
```

● base-infra.yml

```
    ---
    # This playbook deploys components needed for the Infrastructure
hosts.

    hosts: hosts
    remote_user: root
    become: true
    roles:
     - create-nagios-user
     - infra-plugin-config
```

● post-nagios-install.yml

```
    ---
    # This playbook deploys components needed for NConf.

    hosts: nagios-server
    remote_user: root
    become: true
    roles:
     - nagios-post-install
```

Finally, in the end, we have created the hosts file, which also is located in the root
directory of the playbook directory:

```
[nagios-server]
021579-nagios01
```

The complete set of code can again be found in the following GitHub
repository at
`https://github.com/os-admin-with-ansible/os-admin-with-ansible-v2/tree/master/nagios-openstack`.

Before we finish up this topic, we of course need to test out our work and add in some
additional instructions to complete the Nagios setup. At the end of running these playbooks
and roles, you will have a powerful monitoring machine for your OpenStack clouds and
other applications. Assuming that you have cloned the GitHub repository earlier, the
command to test out the playbook from the Deployment node will be as follows:

1. Move the playbooks and roles into the OSA deployment directory.

    In order to leverage the dynamic inventory capabilities that come with OSA, the
    playbooks and roles need to be local to the deployment directory. Trust me you
    will like this!

    ```
    $ cd os-admin-with-ansible-v2/nagios-openstack
    $ mkdir /opt/openstack-ansible/playbooks/groups_vars
    $ cp ~/nagios-openstack/group_vars/* /opt/openstack-
    ansible/playbooks/group_vars
    $ cp -r ~/nagios-openstack/roles/* /opt/openstack-ansible/roles
    $ cp ~/nagios-openstack/base* /opt/openstack-ansible/playbooks
    $ cp ~/nagios-openstack/hosts /opt/openstack-ansible/playbooks
    ```

2. Execute the following playbook to install and configure SNMP on your OSA
    cloud:

    ```
    $ cd /opt/openstack-ansible/
    $ openstack-ansible -i inventory/dynamic_inventory.py
    playbooks/base.yml
    ```

If the SNMP service does not start the first time, please execute the
following commands:

```
$ ansible all_containers -m shell -a "service snmpd start"
$ ansible hosts -m shell -a "service snmpd start"
```

3. Execute the following playbook to install and configure Nagios onto your
    monitoring server:

    ```
    $ cd playbooks
    $ openstack-ansible -i hosts base-nagios.yml
    ```

Then connect to the monitoring server via SSH to execute the following commands to set the *nagiosadmin* user password (used to log in to Nagios web dashboard) and restart Nagios:

```
$ cd /etc/nagios3
$ sudo htpasswd -c /etc/nagios3/htpasswd.users nagiosadmin
$ service nagios3 restart
```

4. Execute the following playbook to install and configure NConf onto your monitoring server:

```
$ openstack-ansible -i hosts base-nconf.yml
```

   1. **NConf initial configuration**: My attempt to automate this part was not successful, so you have to finish the NConf configuration using the NConf web console. Browse http://<monitoring server IP>/nconf and follow the prompts to complete the initial configuration. Here are the suggested inputs and keep the defaults for the others:

```
DBNAME: same as what you inputed in the variables file above
DBUSER: same as what you inputed in the variables file above
DBPASS: same as what you inputed in the variables file above
NCONFDIR: /var/www/html/nconf
NAGIOS_BIN: /usr/sbin/nagios3
```

   2. **Execute the post NConf playbook**:

```
$ openstack-ansible -i hosts post-nconf-install.yml
```

5. Execute the following playbook to configure the OSA nodes to allow for monitoring via SSH:

In order to monitor the OpenStack processes and APIs running on the local containers, you must run the service checks remotely over SSH. The good news is that the Nagios plugin to do this already exists (check_by_ssh):

```
$ cd ..
$ openstack-ansible -i
  inventory/dynamic_inventory.py
  playbooks/base-infra.yml
```

      • Confirm the Nagios and NConf installation: in a browser, go to the following URLs:

           • http://<monitoring server IP>/nagios3

           • http://<monitoring server IP>/nconf

6. Time to configure Nagios for monitoring OSA.

Unfortunately, this part does require manual configuration as each installation will differ too much to automate. In the big picture, this will just help you sharpen your Nagios skills. Do not worry; a copy of the Nagios directory was already taken. This step will take some time and should not be rushed.

The first step here is to customize the Nagios configuration files located in the `/etc/nagios3/rpc-nagios-configs` directory on your monitoring server. All the configuration files are important, but the most critical ones are the `advanced_services.cfg` and `hosts.cfg` files.

Within the `advanced_services.cfg` file, you will need to update each service check with the IP addresses of the containers within your OSA install. The fastest way to get that information is to execute the following command and capture the output on each infrastructure node: `lxc-ls --fancy`. Here is an example:

```
define service {
  service_description    infra1_check_ssh_process_glance-api
  check_command          check_by_ssh_process!<glance container
                         IP>!glance-api
  check_period           24x7
  notification_period    24x7
  host_name              <OSAD node name>
  contact_groups         +admins,rpc-openstack-support
  use                    rpc-service
}
```

The same goes for the `hosts.cfg` file; please update the OSA node names and IP addresses:

```
define host {
  host_name              <OSAD node name>
  address                <OSAD node IP>
  icon_image_alt         Ubuntu 14.04
  icon_image             base/ubuntu.gif
  statusmap_image        base/ubuntu.gd2
  check_command          check-host-alive
  check_period           24x7
  notification_period    24x7
  contact_groups         +admins,rpc-openstack-support
  use                    rpc-node
}
```

[206]

Please also add the following to the bottom of the `resources.cfg` file located in the root of the Nagios directory (`/etc/nagios3`):

```
$USER10$=<random SNMP community string of your choice, keep it
simple>
```

If you are having trouble making the updates to the configurations using an editor, do not stress out as the next step will make this process a bit easier.

7. Import Nagios configuration into NConf

Next appended the contents of the configuration files in the `/etc/nagios3/rpc-nagios-configs` directory to the current Nagios configuration files (add to bottom). Every host, host group, check, service, and contact group is uniquely named so as not to conflict with the current Nagios setup. Then, we will step through the instructions found on the NConf website, `http://www.nconf.org/do kuwiki/doku.php?id=nconf:help:how_tos:import:import_nagios`.

As the NConf tutorial suggests, first run the commands with the `-s` parameters to simulate the import process first. After being able to run with no errors, remove the `-s` parameter to do the final import. Having connected to the monitoring server via SSH, run the following commands:

```
$ cd /var/www/html/nconf
$ bin/add_items_from_nagios.pl -c
  timeperiod -f /path/to/timeperiods.cfg -s
$ bin/add_items_from_nagios.pl -c
  misccommand -f /path/to/misccommands.cfg -s
$ bin/add_items_from_nagios.pl -c
  checkcommand -f
  /path/to/checkcommands.cfg -s
$ bin/add_items_from_nagios.pl -c contact -f
  /path/to/contacts.cfg -s
$ bin/add_items_from_nagios.pl -c
  contactgroup -f
/path/to/contactgroups.cfg -s
$ bin/add_items_from_nagios.pl -c
  host-template -f
/path/to/host_templates.cfg -s
$ bin/add_items_from_nagios.pl -c
  service-template -f
  /path/to/service_templates.cfg -s
$ bin/add_items_from_nagios.pl -c hostgroup -f
  /path/to/hostgroups.cfg -s
$ bin/add_items_from_nagios.pl -c host -f
```

```
    /path/to/hosts.cfg -s
$ bin/add_items_from_nagios.pl -c advanced-
    service -f /path/to/advanced-services.cfg -s
```

Now you can edit all the Nagios configurationss within the NConf web console.

8. Execute the post Nagios playbook:

```
$ cd playbooks
$ openstack-ansible -i hosts post-nagios-
install.yml
```

9. Generate your first Nagios config

Once you are satisfied with all of your custom Nagios configurations (trust me that you will do this a couple of times), click on the **Generate Nagios config** link on the sidebar of the NConf web console. It will note if any errors were encountered. From time to time, you will see warnings, and they are just warnings, nothing urgent.

Last but not the least, from the monitoring server, execute the following command to deploy the Nagios configurations to Nagios (may need to use sudo):

```
$ cd /var/www/html/nconf/ADD-ONS
$ ./deploy_local.sh
```

Summary

Having a rock solid monitor platform on your side is the key to cloud success (actually any production systems success). Remember that this is only a starting point. I expect you to improve/customize it for your specific needs. I am looking forward to seeing all your great work in the future. Please make sure to share any changes you make, remember Open Source is all about sharing. Before wrapping up this final chapter, let's take a moment to recap what we discussed. First we covered some monitoring tips and tricks. Then examined the OpenStack components worth monitoring. Next, we learned how to use Ansible ad hoc commands. We then transitioned into how to set up Nagios and import the custom plugins for the service checks. Finally, we developed Ansible playbooks and roles to automate the base installation of Nagios and NConf with customizing it to completely monitor an OpenStack cloud.

Well ladies and gentleman, this has been fun and honestly a privilege to be allowed to share these automation examples with you for the second time around. Please keep up the great work and also keep an eye out for future revisions as both OpenStack and Ansible continues to mature. I am really looking forward to hearing your feedback and seeing how you took these examples to the next level.

Index

CPSIA information can be obtained
at www.ICGtesting.com
Printed in the USA
FSHW04n1900260318
46055FS